After God's Own Heart:
THE LIFE AND FAITH OF DAVID

Randy L. Hyde

Foreword by John Killinger

PublishAmerica
Baltimore

First printing

All quotations, except where noted, come from the New Revised Standard Version of the Bible.

ISBN: 1-4137-6612-9
PUBLISHED BY PUBLISHAMERICA, LLLP
www.publishamerica.com
Baltimore

Printed in the United States of America

Dedicated to
Alexander Raines,
in whose presence I cannot help but find joy,
and to
Matthew Thomas,
whose presence itself is gift

To my friend Edie –
Thank you for sharing your
hearts with me –

Gratefully,

Rand Hyde

Acknowledgments

I would not have been able to complete this manuscript had it not been for the support and kindness of the following people:

My wife Janet, who has been by my side since 1970. She has always been an encourager to me, and is the one person I know more than any other who is after God's own heart...

My congregation, the Pulaski Heights Baptist Church in Little Rock, Arkansas. They had never before granted a pastor the opportunity of a sabbatical, but graciously did so in my case after the appropriate seven years. I would not have been able to complete this book had it not been for this significant time away

My former professor and life-long friend, John Killinger, who has authored many books and encouraged me in this endeavor, and who graciously agreed to write the foreword...

My friend Mike McCoy, whose drawing graces the cover...

Eugene Peterson, whom I have never met. His book, *Leap Over the Wall*, is cited several times here, and inspired me to delve into David's life, something I had not done before on such a large scale.

And finally, the good people of the Lilly Foundation, whose generosity toward me and those of my profession made this sabbatical possible.

Contents

Preface		7
Foreword by John Killinger		8
One	The Chosen	11
Two	Trusting God	18
Three	The Wilderness Places of Life	26
Four	The Mighty Have Fallen	34
Five	The Context of Salvation	41
Six	A Long Stride and a Large Embrace	48
Seven	God in a Box	55
Eight	When God Says No	64
Nine	Justice and Equity	70
Ten	Sent	78
Eleven	Son of David	83

Preface

David. Just the mention of his name brings immediate recognition. Ask even the biblically uninitiated what first comes to mind when David's name is cited and Goliath will roll off the tongue. Of course, there is much more to this complex man than just his moment of glory in slaying the Philistine warrior. Yet, people are aware of him, if for no other reason than he met the giant in the valley of Elah and came out the winner.

Go with him beyond his victory at Elah and you will find that every page of the Old Testament record reveals a different layer to David, the first true royal leader of Israel. The more you read, the more complex David becomes. So allow me to offer this disclaimer now…No book can do him justice, nor fully explain who he was or describe the impact he has had on the world.

Did you know there is more biblical information and narrative material on David, the son of Jesse, than on anyone else in all of scripture, including Jesus? Trying to capture the mind and heart of this man is a daunting task, but well worth the effort. Why? Because, to understand even something of the life of David is to have a more thorough grasp of God's intention in the life of Israel. To understand how God has woven his will through his people is to be aware of God's salvation purposes for his entire creation. In other words, understanding David is key to comprehending all of scripture and the plan of God for the ages.

That makes this effort very personal. It would be most difficult to emerge from a study of David without being changed by it. And that is why delving into David's heart and life is worth the effort!

With any endeavor like this, there is the risk of transmitting one's twenty-first century mindset into the Mideast world of three millennia ago. But that is the nature of scripture. It weaves and moves its way through the years and the lives of those who find inspiration in its pages. With its ancient stories of faith, and of real flesh-and-blood people who were so different from us, the Bible continues to inspire us and therefore reveal the heart of God. May we all be drawn closer to God's heart because we have sought to understand this complex man named David.

Randy L. Hyde
Isle of Iona, Scotland
July 2003

Foreword
by John Killinger

I hadn't read far in the manuscript of this book when I realized what a treat it was to be seeing the saga of King David again through the eyes of a man for whom it was all as real and important as anything happening in the world today.

Contemporary newspapers are filled with accounts of wars, terrorist acts, institutional failures, natural disasters, political blunders, judicial shortcomings, and individual crimes. They are all real, unfortunately, and they have legs. That is, many of them will continue to affect our world for weeks and years to come – perhaps even centuries.

But Randy Hyde realizes that the story of David, even though it was set in a time when people fought with swords and spears instead of guns and Humvees, is as fresh now as it was when it was first told – and that it will continue to be relevant and to influence people's lives long after the events in today's newspaper have been forgotten.

I was shocked recently to hear Professor Amy-Jill Levine of Vanderbilt University Divinity School, where I once taught and Randy earned his Doctor of Ministry degree, say that David might very well have been a mythical character and not a real one at all. I had never heard or suspected that, and I would need to know a lot more of the professor's evidence before I could begin to agree with such an assertion.

Yet I am not sure it would make a lot of difference if David hadn't existed. The stories about him would still be gripping and, in a sense, even true. That is, they would be so true to human experience of life that they would still capture our attention, as they do in this book, and cause us to reflect on the nature and consequences of the actions they represent. And they would be valuable to us, for that reason, as guides for our own moral and spiritual choices.

Randy Hyde, it should be said for those who don't know him, is an avid sportsman. It is a wonder that he became a minister and not a professional golfer or baseball player. I have never known a man who could consistently hit a ball farther or straighter than Randy. He does it with so much grace and ease that he makes it appear deceptively simple.

And if there is any one kind of illustration that prevails more than all the others in this book, it is the sports story or allusion to athletics – the likening of some action in David's life to an event on the golf course or the gridiron or the basketball court that immediately lets the reader know what it was like to be there and see the young shepherd or great warrior or old king in lifelike motion.

I like this, because it is a connection between the real world of David (regardless of whether David himself was real) and the real world where we live today. And it is a real connection. That is, it is a connection in which there exists a rare kind of kinetic energy, enabling us to feel what is happening with a true sense of its reality, a sense felt in our blood and bones and muscles and not merely in our intellects.

Randy is that kind of person. He sees and feels things *actively*, not passively. He combines, in his own experience of the world, both the body and the soul of events. There is a wholeness about him that is often missing in religious figures. He animates the old biblical stories with a sense of their happening now, in his physical appearance as well as in his mind, so that we actually feel what he is trying to tell us. Our eyes narrow, our muscles tense, our arms and legs twitch as we respond to his prose.

It is an extraordinary achievement. In the end, we see what Randy has seen in the narrative of David's life, and follow that narrative to conclusions in our own lives. David's story becomes ours.

And there are probably few things more helpful than a role model like David who, whether he is behaving admirably or despicably – he does both, of course – is being as thoroughly human as it is possible for any of us to be. We need such models in a world as confusing as ours.

And if I am not mistaken, it will grow only more confusing, not less, as the years go by.

~ One ~
The Chosen

*"Do not look on his appearance or on the height of his stature...
for the Lord does not see as mortals see; they look on the
outward appearance, but the Lord looks on the heart"* (1
Samuel 16:7).

His father didn't even call him by his name. Did you notice that? He
didn't even call him by his name.

Samuel, the man of God, is on a mission to find a new king, and God has
promised him the new leader of Israel would come from the loin of Jesse, the
man from Bethlehem. Samuel has set out on this holy mission to find a new king,
a journey that brings him to this small, rather insignificant village about five
miles south of Jerusalem. Upon seeing him enter their town, the elders become
nervous. "Why would Samuel come to see us?" After all, when a man of God
comes to town, trouble usually follows. But Samuel assures them he has come
for no other reason than to make a sacrifice and worship with the people.

It's not exactly the truth, just a little white lie to cover up his real agenda.
Samuel, the man of God, has got something up his sleeve, and a secret to keep,
at least for the time being. Besides, it's really God's secret, not his, and if it
takes a falsehood to keep it so, perhaps God will forgive him. Samuel is looking
for a king, and God has told him the king will come from the man named Jesse.
But he's got to keep it quiet. Okay, okay, truth be told, he lies to protect himself.
If Saul finds out, he will have Samuel's head on a platter. And how is he going
to find a king if that happens?

King Saul, the first king of Israel, has fallen out of favor with God and
it's time for a new king to be anointed. Samuel is God's appointed prophet and
priest, so God sends him out to find the new king and anoint him on the spot.

11

Evidently, Samuel's discerning ability does not exactly top the charts. He has proven himself not to be a good maker of decisions. His sons have gotten out of control and he does little or nothing to take care of that bad situation. He anoints Saul as king, and Saul becomes a major disappointment, to the point that Samuel is grieving over that situation long after the time for grief is over.

And it's proven again here in Bethlehem. Had Samuel been making the decision by himself, he would no doubt have chosen Eliab, the oldest son of Jesse. He is caught up in what John Claypool calls "the 'beauty cult' approach to establishing human worth."[1] So God becomes directly involved in the selection of the new king. God is looking for a man after his own heart, and cannot trust Samuel to make the choice. God has to make it himself.

Like cattle, all the sons of Jesse have been paraded before the man of God, starting with Eliab. Eliab is the tall, dark-headed, handsome, eldest son of Jesse the Bethlehemite. But Eliab isn't the one Samuel is looking for, even though, when he first sees the strapping young man, he is convinced he has found his new king. But Samuel isn't in charge here; God is. All the while, God is whispering instructions in Samuel's ear, "I know Eliab is a big, strong, good-looking lad, but he won't do, Samuel, he just won't do. Saul is big, strong, and good-looking too, and you see what he's become. Keep looking, Samuel, keep looking."

Samuel considers Abinadab, the next son in line. "No," God says, "he's not the one." How about Shammah, son number three? "No, he's not what I'm looking for." They go through the other four sons and God isn't pleased with them either. "I've seen the sons of Jesse," God says to Samuel, "and I don't think there's a royal prospect in the whole bunch."

So Samuel says to God, "That's it. That's all the sons of Jesse. We've wasted our time. Let's go home."

"Not just yet," God says. "Don't be in such a hurry. Samuel, my good friend and trusted servant, you give up too easily. Ask Jesse if he has another son."

So Samuel says to Jesse, "Are all your sons here?"

"Well, no. Not really. There remains yet the youngest, but surely he doesn't count. Besides, he is keeping the sheep."

"Ah," God whispers into Samuel's ear, "that's what I thought. Let's take a look at him, Samuel. Call for the youngest son of Jesse."

"The youngest." That's what Jesse calls his son. "The youngest." He doesn't even call his son by his name.

I know what it's like to be the youngest. I don't have seven brothers, but I am the youngest of three sons. Three is enough, believe me. And, I know what it's like to be called the baby of the house. But I was never treated like Jesse treats David. At least my dad calls me by my name. My parents always made me feel as if I was just as important as my two older brothers. When my mom wanted me, she did go through the litany of names before she ever got to mine…"Hugh, uh Steve, uh Randy…" I heard that all my life. In fact, I still do, but never do I recall being referred to simply as "the youngest," not even by my older brothers. And let me tell you, they could pick on me with the best of them. They still do during the infrequent times we are all together. Once the baby of the family, always the baby of the family. But at least they call me by my name.

Poor David. The Hebrew word used by Jesse carries with it a sense of insignificance, of not counting for very much. Later narratives tell us that this is also pretty much the attitude of David's older brothers toward the youngest of Jesse's sons.

"Are all your sons here?" Samuel persists, not necessarily because he wants to, but because God insists on seeing every son of Jesse. Every last one.

I get a picture in my mind, don't you? It's as if God, unseen to all the rest, is looking over Samuel's shoulder and whispering in his ear. "Nope, nope, nope. Not Eliab. Nope, not Abinadab either. No, I don't care for Shammah. He's definitely not royal material. Keep going, Samuel. Nope, keep going. Keep going. Nope, nope, nope."

"Are all your sons here?"

"Yes…well, no. No, there remains yet the youngest, but he is keeping the sheep." Are you getting the feeling that in Jesse's eyes David doesn't count for much? That may very well be why he's keeping the sheep. It was a job reserved for the lowest of the low, and being the youngest of eight sons and the youngest of ten children altogether, David got the job that was left over — tending the smelly old sheep.

Seven older brothers and two sisters. That was David's familial legacy. Think about this now…If there had been an average of one-and-a-half to two years between them, and given that they all had the same mother, Eliab, the oldest of Jesse's sons would have probably been at least thirty years of age or older. That's a big, big difference between him and his little brother who was probably a young teenager at best. They might not have even known each other very well, Eliab and…what's-his-name. David is the bottom rung on a long, tall ladder.

There seems to be something in the mind of Jesse, and probably the rest

13

of the family too, that makes David seem insignificant to him. David is the youngest, the runt of the litter, good for little else than tending the sheep.

In light of David's place in his family, and the obvious feelings the others had toward him, could it be that there is at least a little bit of David in all of us? This may be the point at which many of us connect with David the most. We may not be the youngest in our families, but we carry around within ourselves these feelings of insignificance. Our feelings about ourselves, at least sometimes, are reduced to the lowest common denominator.

A scene in Stephen Spielberg's movie *Amistad* depicts two men of different cultures and tongues, trying to communicate with one another through an interpreter. Roger Baldwin, played by Matthew McConaughey, speaks English. Cinque, played by Djimon Hounsou, speaks the Mende language. At one point, Baldwin says to Cinque, "Well, I shouldn't have. I shouldn't have."

The interpreter tells him there is a problem. "I can't translate that," he says.

"Why not?" Baldwin asks.

"Because there isn't a word for 'should' in Mende. Either you do something or you don't."[2]

"Should" may be a perfectly good word. We all use it, don't we? But there are times when I wish certain other words weren't in our language. Sometimes I wish the word "just" was not a part of our vocabulary, though the "find-and-replace" feature on my word processor tells me I have already used it four times in this chapter! One of our church members, who directs a neighboring church-related pre-school and is called upon sometimes to pray in staff meetings, told me she was once teased by the pastor for her "wejus" prayers. "What is a 'wejus' prayer?" she asked. "Lord, *wejus* ask you to do this, *wejus* ask you to do that." "Wejus prayers."

It got me to thinking. The word "just" is a *reducing* word. Eugene Peterson refers to it as a "minimizing adjective."[3] When we use it, we are backing off from whatever it is we are talking about. When we say, "I just don't know," what we really mean is, "I don't know, but I'm not quite willing to make a full commitment to my lack of knowledge." Or how about this one: "I just can't do it." We really mean we don't think we can do it or don't want to do it, but we're willing for someone to try and talk us into it if they want to invest their energy in us. Or, if you want to consider it in the context of prayer: "Lord, we just thank you..." Why do we *just* thank God? Why can't we simply thank God? You see, *just* is a *reducing* word, and many times serves absolutely no useful purpose.

That is at the heart of what Jesse says to Samuel. "Oh, I do have another son, that's true. But he's *just* the youngest. You wouldn't be interested in him. He's so insignificant we've got him down on the south forty tending the sheep." What Jesse doesn't seem to know — or really care about — is that the industrious David is using his shepherding experience to learn such "minor" skills as fending off lions and bears for whom a sheep is a three-course meal. And don't forget this one: he's got a slingshot in his hip pocket, and he's getting pretty good with it. He has lots of time to practice. The word "just" may be in Jesse's vocabulary, but you won't find his youngest son David using it.

Jesse and his older sons are working hard to make sure David is considered *just* an ordinary person. But that is a designation David refuses to consider for himself, and it is definitely not the way God looks at him. Why? Because, as God points out to Samuel, "The Lord does not see as a mortal sees; mortals see only appearances but the Lord sees into the heart." It is one of the most incisive statements in all of scripture. "The Lord does not see as a mortal sees; mortals see only appearances but the Lord sees *into the heart*."

If you've perused the table of contents of this book, you will have noted there are eleven chapters. To be honest, there could have been more. After all, as we have mentioned, there is more biblical material devoted to David than anyone else in scripture, including Jesus. But regardless of how much time and energy we spend on this man's story, even if we dissect every jot and tittle of his life, we will always come back to this powerful, powerful affirmation that runs throughout all the scriptures. "The Lord does not see as a mortal sees; mortals see only appearances but the Lord sees into the heart." "The Lord sees into the heart."

You see, it doesn't matter if David is the oldest, the youngest, or somewhere in between. He is the chosen one of God. And when God places his hand upon David's shoulder and says, "You are the one, I have chosen you," all the other criteria, that we tend to think important, mean nothing. Being the oldest, the handsomest, the tallest, the smartest, the most popular doesn't count when God has made up his mind.

There is a story about a group of tourists visiting a picturesque village. One of the tourists sights an old man sitting beside a fence. He walks up to the elderly gentleman and asks him, in a rather patronizing way, "Were any great men born in this village?" The old man looks him in the eye and replies, "Nope, only babies."

There are no instant heroes. Greatness takes time and patience and hard work, not to mention a great deal of courage. David was not born with any of these attributes. He developed them in the face of some rather difficult odds, not the least of which, it seems, is that he was the only one who truly believed in himself. The only one, that is, except God. God had him pegged from the very beginning.

It is my hope that you will do more than read this book; indeed, that you will invest in studying the life of David. If it is true that there is at least a bit of David in all of us, it might, at least at times, be like reading our own biography. But I have to warn you: it is not an "easy read." God's purposes for David, and therefore God's purposes for his people Israel, are often hidden and lurking between the lines. The kind of people God uses to do his will — the supporting cast, if you will — from our modern, more enlightened perspective, are not the most redemptive in the world. The events central to and surrounding the life of David are awkward and raw because David himself is awkward and raw. The pilgrimage through David's life is a tough journey. But it is worth it. Why? Because it is our life journey. It is our story. We are David.

And we need to know that David came to prominence and leadership not because he happened to be in the right place at the right time. This was divine intention. God had chosen him. David was, as the scriptures tell us, a man after God's own heart. *Heart*...there's that word again. "The Lord sees into the heart." And that is what God wants more than anything else in all the world, from David and from you and me. God wants to see into our hearts and find there that which is wholly and fully committed to Him.

Jesus is coming up out from the waters of baptism, Matthew tells us, and a Voice echoes down from heaven. "This is my Son, the Beloved, the Chosen, in whom I take delight." Talk about divine intention! Why does God say this? Because he wants to make sure Jesus knows he is God's Chosen? Maybe. Because he wants those standing around to realize the significance of this moment and the Person who is the center of it? Maybe. But could it also be because Jesus of Nazareth has given His heart to God in a way that no other living person ever has or ever will?

Let it not be lost on us that Jesus is descended from David. Continuing to weave the thread that is found in David's story, Jesus gives his heart wholly and completely to God. He too is a man after God's own heart. Indeed, he is God's own beloved Son. He is God's Chosen. And so are you, and so am I; chosen by God to be His children.

Here in this story God is once again establishing a pattern of not doing the obvious. God chooses David, the red-headed runt of the litter. God sends his Son not as a conquering warrior but as the Son of Man to suffer and to die. God is looking for those who will give their whole heart to Him. And now, it falls to us to give our hearts to the One who has given His heart to us. The glory of our faith is that "the Lord does not see as a mortal sees; mortals see only appearances but the Lord sees into the heart."

What does God see in your heart and in mine? Are we willing to follow in the spiritual footsteps of David? Is it our desire to tune our hearts with the purposes of God as Jesus so obviously did? When God comes and calls our name and looks inside our hearts, what will He find? The oil is prepared and the time of anointing is at hand. Thanks be to God.

Notes

[1] John Claypool, *"The Saga of Life: Childhood,"* unpublished sermon, (September 7, 1975).

[2] Cliff Vaughn, *"A Screen of Terms," Ethicsdaily.com* e-newsletter, (September 5, 2000).

[3] Eugene Peterson, *Leap Over a Wall* (Harper: San Francisco, 1997), p. 21.

~ Two ~
Trusting God

"...so that all the earth may know that there is a God in Israel" (1 Samuel 17:46).

It was late February, 1963. I was walking into our local high school gymnasium realizing that I was about to play in the most important basketball game of my life. My duffle bag was loaded with my "armor," and I was ready for battle. Our team was about to face our archrivals in the finals of the Arkansas state junior high basketball tournament. We were playing the game on our home turf, and the interesting thing is that both teams were from the same region. That meant we had already played one another. In fact, we had played our opponents four times: twice during the regular season, once in an invitational tournament, and yet again in the finals of the regional tournament. My team had been fortunate enough to come out on top every time.

When you play a team that often, you get to know the fellows who wear the other colors. Just as I was about to head into our locker room, Dewey Robbins walked over to me. I got the sense that he had been waiting for me, just so he could give me his little speech. "Hyde," he says to me, "you've beaten us four times this year, and every time it's been by a smaller margin. We're going to get you tonight. We're taking that trophy home."

"Well, we'll see," I told him. "We'll see. Good luck, Dewey." I don't remember if I added, "You'll need it," but I don't think I did.

With all of the dancing and jiving, showboating and annoying behavior of today's athletes, trash-talking has been made into an art form. It's a means of modern-day psychological sports warfare. I have a feeling that if you could hear what's being said on the football field or basketball court, you might not want to watch another game. Things have really changed. Back in 1963, if our coach caught us behaving like that, we would have found ourselves riding the bench before you could say, "What's the score?"

But, as much as I don't want to, I have to admit there is biblical precedence for such behavior. You'll find it recorded in the seventeenth chapter of 1 Samuel, and it takes place in the Valley of Elah. There they stand, facing one another, two armies in a classic battlefield confrontation. One army, the Israelites, under the leadership of King Saul, is encamped on a hill overlooking the valley. The other forces, the Philistines, are gathered on the hill of Socoh. The two armies are at a stalemate. In order to make any kind of move at all, one of the armies will have to go down into the valley. That would place them at a distinct disadvantage. So what do they do? Nothing. They hold their ground and talk trash to one another.

"You Israelite dogs, see if your God will get you out of this mess!"

"Hey, you uncircumcised Philistine pigs, come and get us!"

So far, the only skirmish going on in the Valley of Elah is a war of words.

Several years ago my son Tim and I were watching a college football game on television. Deuce McAllister, of the Ole Miss Rebels, ran a punt back eighty-seven yards against Auburn for a very dramatic touchdown. I told Tim, from my personal experience of a long time ago, that you cannot imagine the adrenalin rush you get when you catch a punt or kickoff, tuck that football in your arm, and then head up the field; all the while knowing there are eleven guys on the other team who want to do nothing less than drive you into the ground so deep you feel as if you could grow grass. Not only that, but they've got a head start on you. They're already running at full speed while you're still trying to catch that wobbly ball!

Imagine, then, how it must feel when you are in the army and the other side faces you on the far hill. In between is the valley, soon to be the valley of death for many of your fellow soldiers, maybe even for you. The sound of "Charge!" is given and you rush forward into the waiting weapons of annihilation. Talk about adrenaline! It's hard to imagine, isn't it, what that must have been like.

It was said that the ancient Goths always went over their battle plan twice before they went into battle — once when they were sober, that they should not lack skill; again when they were drunk, that they should not lack courage. I think I understand. I think I understand.

The Israelites have not yet brought themselves to the point they are ready to take on the Philistines. Maybe they aren't drunk enough. So far, at least, it is only a war of words.

So one day, the Philistine giant named Goliath, walks out in front of his troops, and in a voice that only a giant could produce, bellows at the Israelites, "Let's see how big you Israelites talk when a real man confronts you." He then issues them a challenge. They are to send a man against him. Whoever wins the one-on-one competition will claim the victory for his people. The losers will serve the victors. How's that for trash talk? Suddenly, the Israelite army grows very, very quiet. No more talk of "Philistine pigs." No more screaming across the Valley of Elah.

And that's the way it goes. For forty days, every day at the same time, Goliath issues his challenge to the Israelites forces. You would think that forty days would be enough time for Goliath and his buddies to realize they would get no takers from the ranks of Saul. What no one knows is that, in keeping with God's plan, they are simply waiting for David.

It appears to be a magnanimous gesture on the part of Goliath. "Let one of yours fight me. Whoever loses will serve the other. No more bloodshed. Only one man will die."

Yeah, right. And pigs can fly. He knows it would be the start of a major bloodbath. He knows that the one who is victorious — and he isn't betting on the other guy — would have the upper hand in the fierce battle that ensues. Goliath is playing a psychological game of his own before the real battle starts. It is a hollow promise, and the Israelites, who were not born yesterday, see right through it.

But they also don't know what to do about it. And that includes their leader Saul. We are told previously that "the spirit of the Lord departed from Saul" (16:14). What a terrible thing to happen to anybody. Does Saul know that, or is he left to wallow alone in his delusional paranoia and fear, thinking all the while that the God of Israel is on his side? Whatever we may think of this tragic statement, Saul doesn't have a clue as to what to do with this nine-foot-tall enemy swearing at him from across the valley. Saul, along with the rest of his army, is frozen in fear.

And along comes little David, the teenage youngest son of Jesse, patriarch of a large but common family in a remote and insignificant village. David has come to bring provisions to his three oldest brothers who are serving in Saul's army.

As with everything else, warfare has evolved through the ages. The way war is conducted now is greatly removed from the way it was done just thirty-something years ago in Vietnam, and certainly in Iraq. Think of how it has changed since David-and-Goliath days. Saul's army is really nothing more than a "people's militia."[1] The attitude of war, as it is recorded in the Old Testament, is more closely related to the way battles were conducted during the War Between the States when they simply lined up across from one another and charged, rather than our "surgical strike," computerized form of battle today.

I write these words as my wife Janet and I are on sabbatical in Scotland. Scotland has a long and rather bloody history, and we have witnessed evidences of it. We have bowed our heads at Culloden, where the misguided efforts of Bonnie Prince Charlie came to a bloody, ignominious conclusion and forever ended the Stuart aspirations of reclaiming the British throne. Culloden's holy ground is littered with mounds, formed by the mass burials of those who died so needlessly. We have visited the William Wallace Monument in Stirling, and climbed its 247 narrow, winding steps — twice! We have walked the grounds of Bannockburn where Robert the Bruce's forces, inspired by carrying a cask containing the bones of St. Andrew into battle, defeated the armies of Edward II.

What success the Scots did have in securing freedom from the English was by means of something unique for that day, not witnessed ever before. The Scots used guerrilla warfare. Wallace's forces did not defeat the English in an open field, as portrayed in the movie *Braveheart*. They waited until the English were crossing Stirling Bridge, and then slaughtered them in the bogs below. Yet, it is true that generally, when armies faced one another, they did so by simply lining up against one another and having at it.

That was just as true in the days of the Israelites when they had the misfortune to serve under the questionable leadership of King Saul. The prospects of doing so were not exactly burning bright, and it appears that no one, even Saul, wants anything to do with it.

David arrives just as another verbal skirmish is about to begin, and he is eager to get in on the action. He is just young and naive enough to be fascinated by war, rather than repelled by it. When he hears the taunts of the giant Goliath, he is offended, not only by what the giant says and does, but by what his fellow countrymen don't do. They've heard the boasting of the giant for forty days now. David is hearing it for the first time. No doubt following the attitude of their king, which is totally lacking in spiritual direction, the Israelites act as if God has nothing to do with the situation with which they are faced.

That is not the way David thinks or operates. Immediately, he brings God into the equation. "Who is this uncircumcised Philistine that he should defy the armies of the living God?" If God is not with the Israelites, the giant is right.

There is nothing to be done. But for David, it is unthinkable to deal with life's difficulties without consideration of God's purpose and plan in it.

David is viewed, not only by Saul's soldiers but also his own brothers, as impudent; which, of course, he is. Have you ever encountered a teenager who had all the answers? Better question: have you ever encountered a teenager who *didn't* have all the answers? There is no more obnoxious creature in all the earth. I know, I used to be one, and I've raised two. I can barely remember being a teenager myself, but I'm still reminded of it occasionally by my older brothers (see chapter one!). The teenager, David, is carrying around with him, not only his slingshot but an obnoxious faith as well, if there is such a thing. And what is perceived as an arrogant attitude doesn't go over very well with the older, more experienced soldiers to whom he is posing his question.

Except, oddly enough, King Saul. When he hears of David and his willingness to take on the giant, he is intrigued. He is obviously desperate and grasping at straws.[2] The king gives an audience to the young shepherd when no one else, it seems, wants to listen to him.

But wait a minute. Let's get this royal protocol thing straight. Isn't it true that when you visit with royalty, you do not speak until first spoken to? Not David. Remember, he has all the answers. Without waiting to hear what the king has to say, he, like Goliath, does some bellowing of his own. "Do not lose heart because of this arrogant Philistine. I, your servant, will go and fight him."

How did David know Saul had lost heart? Could he see it in his face? Maybe he misinterpreted the expression Saul had given him.

Let's try to put ourselves in Saul's place. The Philistine giant has got his troops quaking at the knees. In fact, his are beginning to feel a bit like Jell-o as well. He gets word that there is at last someone who is willing to take on Goliath, and he begins to have some hope. However, when the willing warrior walks into his tent he turns out to be just a boy! His feelings of relief give way to utter disappointment, and surely his face reveals it. David may have taken that to mean Saul is disheartened, and in fact he is…not just by the bragging presence of the giant, but that the only soldier he has who is willing to fight Goliath isn't even one of his soldiers. He's *just* a young boy whose face has never even seen a razor!

"You can't go up against the Philistine," Saul says. "Why, you're, you're *just* a boy! The giant has been a warrior all his life. He was fighting battles before you were a smile on your mother's face. How in the world do you think you can take on such a man as he? Look at him, son, look at him. His arm is bigger than you. Why, you're *just* a boy!"

Remember that word *just*? All his life people have used the word *just* with David. His father used it, his brothers used it, and you can bet that even when Samuel was pouring the anointing oil over his head, making David the new king, the new wave of Israel's future, David could hear the old man muttering, "Lord, do you know what you're doing? He is *just* a boy, and not a very big one at that. You want *him* to be king over Israel? I've never doubted you before, Lord, but don't you think this is a bit much?" And now, David is hearing it again. Oh, how he has come to hate that word *just*. If he never hears it again he will be the happiest guy in all Judea. As far as David is concerned, doubting him is the same as doubting God, for he was a man — okay, at this point a boy — after God's own heart.

"I've slain lions and bears," he tells Saul. "This uncircumcised Philistine, in my hands, will fare no better." And then we are given a clue as to David's great faith. He has confidence that he will slay Goliath, not because he's smarter or quicker or has better fighting skills. His confidence is not in himself, it is in his God. He is convinced that Goliath will fall this day because "he has defied the armies of the living God." And that, to David's way of thinking, is a capital offense.

Where did David get such incredible confidence, not to mention verbal ability, that he was able to proclaim this kind of speech to his king? By preaching to his sheep? Where did David get such tremendous faith, that he was willing to stand before the fierce Goliath, evidently without fear? By fighting lions and bears?

There is a key word in this story that bears consideration. It is the word *deliver*. It may sound like trash talk, but the truth is, this is David's declaration of faith. "This very day the Lord will *deliver* you into my hand, and I will strike you down and cut off your head; and I will give the dead bodies of the Philistine army this very day to the birds of the air and to the wild animals of the earth, so that all the earth may know that there is a God in Israel, and that all this assembly may know that the Lord does not save by sword and spear; for the battle is the Lord's and he will give you into our hand."

You see, Saul and his people had forgotten there was a God in Israel, and it took David to remind them. Just as God had delivered the lion and the bear into his hand, he would deliver the giant. Whatever fear David may have had, the living God of Israel has delivered him from it. David is a man after God's own heart, and he proves it that day in the Valley of Elah.

And King Saul says, "Go, and may the Lord be with you." He utters

God's name, but he cannot bring himself fully to trust in God. How do we know? Look at what he does next. He tries to put his own armor on David. His faith is still in that which is fashioned by human hands. He is trying to add to David's weight, and David has been busy divesting himself of all which would encumber him. He leaves his flock of sheep, he deposits with the baggage keeper the provisions he has brought to the battle scene for his brothers, and now he sheds Saul's armor. He is prepared to face Goliath with five smooth stones, his courage and wits, and the presence of his living God.

And then he proceeds to do exactly what he told the giant he was going to do. He knocks him to the ground with a stone from his slingshot, dispatches him with his own sword, and cuts off his head. Bang, that's it. We've been waiting for this for forty-seven verses, and suddenly it's over. When the Philistines see that their great warrior is dead, they flee for their lives, only to be overrun by the Israelites who have found new courage through the exploits of David. What a story. What a story. On that fateful day in the Valley of Elah, David slays Goliath.

But, in all honesty, we must admit that Goliath is still alive, even today. Today, the giant Goliath stands before us in different forms. Do we not feel as if we are confronted by a blasphemous giant when we are told the word "cancer"? What about AIDS or Alzheimer's? There are other Goliaths in our land: dead-end jobs, fractured relationships, wayward children…suspicion, anger, crime, dishonesty, vengeance, hate…road rage, jealousy, disregard for the well-being of others. You get the picture, I think. I hope. There is a giant among us, and each of us faces Goliath every day in some form or another. So what do we do? Can we learn a lesson from David? Is there any hope?

Yes, we can and, yes there is. As an act of faith and trust, when faced by Goliath, as David did, we divest ourselves of that which no longer is important, and take into battle only that which is essential. When the doctor says, "cancer," suddenly that sofa you've had your eye on isn't so important anymore, is it? When she says to you, "I want out," that new car no longer holds such an attraction. When you find yourself in conflict, the only thing on your mind and heart is a solution that will bring peace to your soul. You shed the weight of that which is not as important as it used to be.

Why is it that too often we have to be faced with a major crisis before we are willing to do that which brings us back to God? The reason David was prepared to face Goliath is that he brought his great faith with him. He didn't wait to rediscover it when faced with a crisis. What was a paralyzing confrontation to Saul and his troops was just an annoyance to the young shepherd because he brought his faith with him to the Valley of Elah.

David teaches us that we are to abandon our spiritual encumbrances and look to God for deliverance, and not wait until we face Goliath to do so. We are to shed the unnecessary armor that comes with a spirit lacking in faith, and then stand naked before the God in whom we give our trust.

There come those times in life when we know we cannot do it by ourselves anymore. We must give our trust, wholly and completely, to God. So the next time you stand in the Valley of Elah, which might be right now, look up, look up. You will not only see Goliath standing before you, you will witness the mighty army of God. Take heart, my friends, and put your trust in the God who brings deliverance.

Notes

[1] Walter Brueggemann, *Interpretation*: *First and Second Samuel* (John Knox Press: Louisville, Kentucky), p. 128.

[2] Ibid., p. 129.

~ Three ~
The Wilderness Places of Life

"So Saul stopped pursuing David, and went against the Philistines; therefore that place was called the Rock of Escape" (1 Samuel 23:28).

"Then Jesus was led up by the Spirit into the wilderness to be tempted by the devil" (Matthew 4:1).

I'm not exactly a cowboy, but I do have some experience with the American west, both personally and from some rather extensive reading. Hey, all those Louis L'Amour novels ought to count for something, don't you think? Besides, I doubt if anyone gets greater pleasure than I from watching an old "B" western movie…the cornier the better. The crossword puzzles call them "oaters," and I can't think of a better term for them.

From my limited experience I can tell you that there's nothing quite like being in the desert, especially early in the morning when the sun is coming up. The air is clean and crisp and cool, and you can see for miles and miles and miles. There's simply this feeling that comes over you, telling you there's no other place like it in all the earth. You cannot help but feel that the desert holds many secrets, and she isn't willing to tell them all to you. In order to discover what some of those secrets may be, you have to explore and question and probe and seek.

It almost goes without saying that the desert is hauntingly beautiful. But your instinct also tells you the desert is a wildly dangerous place to be. After all, it is the wilderness.

Young David is in the wilderness of life, both literally and figuratively. We have been told that while God's Spirit dwells with David, that same Spirit has departed from Saul, the king of Israel. The relationship between Saul and David has become complex and murderous. Saul, in his paranoia and fear, looks upon David as the enemy, and with a mystifying and inconsistent rage, has made several attempts on David's life. David has no choice but to run from Saul because, while Saul may be insane, he isn't stupid. He currently holds the throne of Israel, and as long as he is the recognized king there will be those who support him and toady up to him. They are perhaps as dangerous as the crazy king himself.

If you've ever read an espionage novel, with its complex twists and turns, you might have a feel for what David is going through. You don't know who is your friend or ally, and those who profess to be may, at any given moment, be plotting with the enemy to take your life. As one pundit has said, "Even a paranoid has his enemies," and David and Saul both know what he means. The only thing for David to do is get out of Dodge, or in old western parlance, "light a shuck"...lay low until things cool off. David flees from Saul, taking his friends with him, and they head for the wilderness.

In the Old Testament book of 1 Samuel, there are fifteen stories recounting David's experiences in the wilderness. It was during this time of his life that David wrote many of the psalms which are attributed to him. Listen to some of the plaintive cries lifted up by David:

> *Why do the nations conspire,*
> *and the peoples plot in vain?*
> *The kings of the earth set themselves,*
> *and the rulers take counsel together*
> *against the Lord and his anointed... (2:1-2).*

> *Give ear to my words, O Lord;*
> *give heed to my sighing.*
> *Listen to the sound of my cry,*
> *my King and my God,*
> *for to you I pray (5:1).*

> *O Lord my God, in you I take refuge;*
> *save me from all my pursuers,*
> *and deliver me (7:1).*

In the Lord I take refuge;
how can you say to me,
"Flee like a bird to the mountains;
for look, the wicked bend the bow,
they have fitted their arrow to the string,
to shoot in the dark at the upright in heart..." (11:1-2).

They sound like the painful words of a man on the run, don't they? But David was doing more than just writing psalms of lament. It was during this time that he continued to hone his fighting and survival skills. However, when a person is going through a wilderness place of life, there is more to the experience than just nursing the pain of it. There is more to it than just surviving it. There comes no good from going through the wilderness unless you also allow it to deepen and sharpen your spiritual sensitivity. And that is exactly what David does. He comes to look upon his enemy Saul, not with hatred and revenge, but with respect, reverence, and yes, even love. And this for a man who has attempted on more than one occasion to pin him against the wall with his spear! This for a man who is as crazy as a loon!

In the previous chapter, in our consideration of David before Goliath, the key word was *deliver*. Here, the focal word is *refuge*. It is the single most important thing you need when you find yourself in the wilderness places of life. When you are drowning, what you need most is air. When you are dying of thirst, that which you crave more than anything else is water. When you are desperate and have the enemy at your heel, the most important thing to you is refuge, a place to rest your weary soul.

David finds refuge, ironically, in his friendship with Jonathan, the son of Saul. He finds refuge through a midmorning escape, made possible by the cunning of his wife Michal, Saul's daughter. Adding to our awareness of Saul's psychological, emotional, and spiritual failures is the fact that his very own family members aid the man whom he considers his greatest enemy. What a commentary on Saul's life! David flees to Nob and is given assistance by the priest Ahimelech, who eventually will pay for it with his life and the lives of almost all in his family...

And David thinks he will also find refuge in the village of Keilah. There he saves the people from the raiding Philistines. And how do they repay him for his bravery and kindness? They betray him to Saul. David escapes and runs to Horesh where the Ziphites live. They too betray him to Saul. Now, it seems, everywhere he turns, David is betrayed by those who have received his benefit. Go figure. In the days of Saul and David, there appears to be no such thing as justice or fairness.

We are not told why the Ziphites have it in their hearts to betray David. Sometimes there simply is no explanation for loyalties or the lack thereof. For example, when two people divorce, is it not generally true that their friends will often choose sides? "It's all his fault." "No, it's all her fault." When conflict besieges a church, some will defend the pastor, who is usually at the center of the firestorm, while others will call for his or her resignation. To try and explain such behavior is usually futile. It happens. It just happens. There are times when our feelings cannot be explained or defended. We simply feel the way we feel and that's the way it is. It is unfortunate, even though God's Spirit has departed from Saul, that the residents of Keilah and the Ziphites come down on the side of Saul against David.

Maybe David's men were less than kind to these people. In conjunction with their Olympics coverage a few years ago, NBC did a feature on a South Sea island invaded by the Japanese during World War II. The incident and the island became rather famous years later because this is where John F. Kennedy's PT 109 was attacked and destroyed. The island natives were more than willing to assist Kennedy and his crewmen in making their escape because the occupying Japanese troops had treated them so cruelly. Maybe the people of Keilah and the Ziphites feel the same way toward David and his men. Being on the lam can make for desperation, and sometimes desperate men — even David's men, perhaps — can be cruel men. It's a possibility, but the truth of the matter is, we don't know.

We do know this…by the time this narrative comes along, Saul's intense and insane hatred of David is firmly established. Somehow, Saul knows that the future leadership of Israel belongs to David, not to him. His son Jonathan said so. This only adds to his lunacy, and the insanity that causes him to seek David's life. And because of that, David is looking for refuge in the only place he can find it — the wilderness.

Did you notice how the writer frames his story? He is very specific about where David's wilderness movements take him: from the Wilderness of Ziph on the hill of Hachilah, which is south of Jeshimon, they reconnoiter to Maon, in the Arabah. Why is the author so specific? Wouldn't it be sufficient simply to say that David was flitting around in the wilderness? Perhaps he wants us to try and get inside the mind of Saul. Now, that's a scary thought, is it not? When he learns that the Ziphites are willing to assist him in finding David, Saul says to them, "Find out exactly where he is, and who has seen him there; for I am told that he is very cunning. Look around and learn all the hiding places where he lurks, and come back to me with sure information."

"The narrative takes us hill-by-hill, cliff-by-cliff, crag-by-crag, rock-by-rock…"[1] through David's wilderness wanderings, giving us a sense of the desperation, not only of David and his men, but of Saul as well, in trying to find them. Desperation runs all through this story and clings to it like clothing soaked with sweat. Saul receives his information from the Ziphites and pursues David. He has him pinned down in the wilderness of Maon. David and his men are on one hill, hiding in the caves, and Saul is on the other hill beating the bushes for his mortal enemy. All the while Saul is getting closer, closer, closer. He is just about to pin down David and his men where they cannot possibly escape.

And then Saul gets word that the Philistines have started raiding again. He is forced to pull back his troops so he can go and fight the real enemy. As much as he hates David — and believe it, he hates David with the darkest of passion — he hates the Philistines even more. Oh, how the Israelites hated the Philistines! It was mutual, I'm sure. And David is saved from the insane antagonism of Saul, at least for the time being. They call that place the Rock of Escape, we are told, for on that fateful day David escaped from his enemy Saul.

It is no wonder that the wilderness has become a metaphor for some of the difficult times we experience in life. Just when we think we've gotten the tiger by the tail, just when we think that maybe we're over the hump and can coast for awhile, just when we start to believe that perhaps life is going to cut us a break, we find ourselves lying prostrate beneath a scorching sun, seeking a drink of water and sucking up only sand. The wilderness is a desperate place to be.

Perhaps you find yourself in the wilderness right now. If that is true, you are certainly not alone.

Each week our church secretary makes copies of the prayer requests our worshipers write on the back of their welcome cards and gives them to me. If the petitioner specifically requests it, she will place these requests in our prayer room as well. More often than not, these prayers are requested for others who are in the wilderness of life. Particularly touching are the prayer requests of our children. On occasion, they have brought tears to my eyes for their simplicity and thoughtfulness, further reinforcing for me that a simple faith is the best kind of faith. Sometimes, however, our parishioners will ask for the prayer support of their church family for themselves. They may not have thought about it with this kind of imagery, but they are finding themselves wandering in the wilderness. They are looking for refuge, and they seek such refuge in the prayers of others. Make no mistake about it: the most powerful force on earth or in heaven is the fervent prayer of a believer cast in intercession for another person.

I think of some good friends of mine who are in the wilderness places of life. One has struggled with breast cancer for several years now, another has just completed his second round of chemotherapy as he fights lymphoma. Another is a pastor and has resigned his pulpit with no place to go. Wilderness places indeed.

My friend and former professor, John Killinger, who has graciously provided a foreword for this book, more than twenty years ago published what has become a devotional classic, *Bread for the Wilderness, Wine for the Journey*. It was re-published a few years ago, and in the foreword to the new edition John, who is a prolific author, says that of all his books which have gone out of print over the years, more people had asked for a re-publication of this one than any other. "Scarcely a month goes by," he says, "that I do not receive a note or a letter asking where the writer may find a copy." He goes on to say that the book needed little, if any, revision. The timeliness of it remained true over two decades despite the changes witnessed in our culture.[2]

Why do you suppose that is, not only that the book needed little revision but that it has struck such a responsive chord with so many people? I have a theory. No matter how much our world may change, and we react to those changes in different and varied ways, there will always be the wilderness places of life reaching up to ensnare us. Sooner or later, the wilderness calls for everybody. Everybody — and this seems especially true for people who place their trust in God — eventually comes to the wilderness places of life. And because the wilderness never dies, we need to know what happens in the wilderness. Because the wilderness never dies, neither does our need for God, the God of redemption and salvation. For you see, not only do we need redemption and salvation for our souls, sometimes our greatest need seemingly has nothing to do with the promise of heaven. We need for God to provide refuge now, right now, through God's intervening Spirit. Sometimes, our greatest need, as evidenced in David's experience, is simply survival. "Stay alert, stay alive — that's it."[3] Sometimes, even when our trust is in God, we find ourselves desperate and clutching for anything that will bring us through the wilderness places of life.

Jesus, too, experienced the wilderness places of life. And it happened to him as it comes to most of us: just when he should have been on top of the world, ready to grab it by the tail. After all, he has just heard the Voice come down from heaven saying, "This is my Son, the Beloved, with whom I am well pleased." He has received the endorsement of God himself. You would think it was time to get on with it.

But what happens? Immediately, Jesus is cast into the wilderness where, for forty days and nights he has nothing to eat or drink. And all the time is tempted by the devil.

There are times, are there not, when we feel Jesus has got nothing on us. You tend to feel that way when the wilderness invades. You are all alone. No one has ever felt as you feel, no one has ever wandered so deeply into the wilderness caves as you now find yourself. No one understands. You are all alone, and not even God answers your calls. That is the wilderness.

If that is true of you right now, consider this...David wasn't the only one in the wilderness of En-gedi. His enemy and pursuer, Saul, was wandering around the desert too. It seems to me that both these men serve as examples of how we can react to the wilderness places of life. In the wilderness we can seek for God and be found by God, as David did; or we can seek the enemy and fail to see God in our experiences, as did Saul.

There is a sense in which David isn't running from Saul as much as he is running to God. While Saul is losing his mind, David is finding God's true purpose for his life. David has taken with him, into the wilderness, a seeking spirit, a desire to determine where it is God wants him to go next. David is searching for God, and Saul, in his insanity, is reduced to seeking only revenge.

When we find ourselves in the wilderness places of life, those appear to be our choices. We can seek God or we can seek revenge.

The wilderness is a beautiful, haunting, dangerous place. And nothing on God's earth will prevent us from it. Eventually, finally, inevitably, each of us will go through the wilderness. When we do, the question we must face is, will we seek God there? If the answer is yes, God will finally turn our wilderness into a place of joy.

Notes

[1]Walter Brueggemann, *Interpretation: 1 and 2 Samuel* (John Knox Press: Louisville, Kentucky, 1990), p. 165.

[2]John Killinger, *Bread for the Wilderness, Wine for the Journey* (Angel Books, Inc.: Centreville, Virginia, 1996), foreword.

[2]Eugene H. Peterson, *Leap Over a Wall* (Harper: San Francisco, 1997), p. 73.

~ Four ~
The Mighty Have Fallen

"They mourned and wept, and fasted until evening for Saul and for his son Jonathan, and for the army of the Lord and for the house of Israel, because they had fallen by the sword" (2 Samuel 1:12).

November, 1963. The morning of Friday, November 22, in fact. I was in the ninth grade. Mrs. Dover was instructing us in algebra when Mrs. Robinson, the school counselor, burst into our classroom shouting, "President Kennedy has been shot! President Kennedy has been shot!" Mrs. Robinson was one of those no-nonsense educator-types who was always in control, and rather stern in her demeanor toward the students. To see her so shaken and emotionally distraught caught us off-guard, so our immediate reaction was more surprise at her behavior than the tragic news she was giving us. It was when we had changed classes and crossed the hall for English that we were told the president had died. Mrs. Summers, our English teacher, led us in a moment of stunned silence. We may have been only fourteen years old, but somehow we understood the impact of that moment. Suddenly, as I recall, the sky turned black and was filled with the sound of thunder and the clash of lightning. It was almost as if God was publicly displaying his personal grief.

Those of you who are old enough to remember, that moment is forever etched in your memory, isn't it? You not only remember, you recall exactly where you were, what you were doing, who you were with. Democrat or Republican, Catholic, Baptist or Jew, our nation found itself suddenly and inexplicably in a deep and mournful grief. Our president, once so young and full of life – the prince of Camelot – was dead.

One of my college roommates, now a pastor in west Little Rock, asked me a few years ago, "Gene Blagg is in your church, isn't he?" When I told him that he is, Clif said, "He was one of my teachers. He's the one who told us that President Kennedy had been assassinated. It seems just like yesterday." You see?

April 4, 1968 — Martin Luther King, Jr., shot by a sniper as he stood on the veranda of the Loraine Hotel in Memphis, Tennessee.

June 5, 1968 — Robert Francis Kennedy, while campaigning in Los Angeles, was shot by Sirhan Sirhan at close range in a hotel kitchen as he was making his exit following a speech.

1968 was a rough year for our nation, wasn't it?

January 28, 1986 — The space shuttle Challenger split the sky and moments later split in two, killing all seven astronauts inside. That flight was of special importance to our nation and the space program because it included the first "layperson" in space, Christa McAuliffe, a schoolteacher from Ohio. I had left my office in Baltimore and was driving to Franklin Square Hospital. Just as I was clearing the parking lot, a news bulletin came over the radio announcing there had been an explosion. I made a u-turn and ran back into my office. Dean Kaufman, my associate, was nearby and I asked him if he had heard the news. He hadn't. He followed me into my office and together we watched the live broadcast on my small television. When the network showed a videotape of the Challenger's short, ill-fated flight, and the explosion that ensued, I remember saying aloud, "They're gone. They're all gone. There's no way they could survive that." For a long time after that, Dean and I sat in stunned silence, watching the coverage without saying a word. Do you remember where you were that day? My guess is you do.

September 11. I don't even have to tell you what year, do I? I suppose it can be said that not anyone famous died that day, but that's hardly the point. Except for a few isolated areas of the world in which hatred runs deep toward those of us in the western world, the earth's population bowed in shock and grief. Where were you that day? Where everyone was: in front of your television set, not believing what you saw, not wanting to believe what you heard.

While in St. Andrews, Scotland, I mentioned the name of Sean Connery, the actor, to our bed-and-breakfast host. "Oh, we all know Sean quite well," he said. "He visits here often." Then, pointing to the couch in his living room, he said, "In fact, he sat right there for hours on 9/11 watching the horrible news with us."

When the mighty have fallen, such moments are frozen in time, are they not? It is the nature of life and of death. When the mighty have fallen, the world — at least our world — stops, and our memories are frozen at that point forever.

The same was true for David. Saul, the first king of Israel, who spent the last years of his life wallowing in the paranoia and fear that comes when God's Spirit has departed...Saul who had become the mortal enemy and pursuer of David...Saul who lusted after David's death more than anything else in life...Saul, David's father-in-law and the father of his best friend, Jonathan...Saul, king of Israel, now lies mortally wounded on Mount Gilboa, having suffered the degrading death of falling on his own sword. He has taken his own life because, having been seriously wounded in battle, he fears death much less than he fears being taken prisoner by the hated Philistines. Jonathan and his two brothers, the three sons of Saul, have also been slain.

It is a dark, dark day for the nation of Israel. The mighty have fallen in battle.

The irony is that it is left to David to lead his people in mourning. It might be thought that David would be more relieved than grieved. Finally, finally, he can come out of the wilderness hills and go home without wondering if the relentless hatred of Saul would finally catch up to him. You might think that ambition swells in his chest. Now he can finally fulfill his destiny as the anointed king of Israel. Saul is out of the way and David can do what he was anointed to do so many years before. It would be the opportune time for David to bring all the attention to himself. But he doesn't do it. His only thoughts are on his old nemesis Saul and his friend Jonathan.

David doesn't feel relief. David isn't heady with ambition. David feels only a deep, deep, genuine sadness and grief. Saul, a great, if not flawed man, the God-anointed leader of his people, has come to his untimely end. Say what you will about David, but his loyalty to Saul as God's anointed king is without question.

David the poet takes over. There is something about grief that causes us to become more reflective than usual.

I remember the Thursday morning in early 1995 when I was driving from our home in northeast Arkansas to Memphis, Tennessee. My wife's father had been in the hospital there for more than a week after suffering a massive stroke. Knowing that he was dying, I thought and prayed as I made my way across the Delta. I remember thinking that life is short and there were a couple of things I had been putting off, things I had really wanted to do, and

I needed to get on with them. When we are confronted with death, we become more open to reflection and contemplation.

In a moment of deep reflection and inspiration, and with a heavy heart, David writes an elegy to Saul and Saul's son, his good friend Jonathan.

> *Thy glory, O Israel, is slain upon thy high places!*
> *How are the mighty fallen!*
> *Tell it not in Gath,*
> *publish it not in the streets of Ashkelon;*
> *lest the daughters of the Philistines rejoice,*
> *lest the daughters of the uncircumcised exult…*
>
> *Saul and Jonathan, beloved and lovely!*
> *In life and in death they were not divided;*
> *they were swifter than eagles,*
> *they were stronger than lions…*
>
> *How are the mighty fallen,*
> *and the weapons of war perished!*

There is no mention here of God, so David's lament was not considered a psalm. It was, however, included in a book of Hebrew poetry called the *Jashar*. Read this portion of 2 Samuel in its entirety, and you cannot help but notice the rhythm of David's lament. The second part of the verse is shorter than the first, creating an imbalance that provides a haunting echo.[1]

It is the same effect you will find when entering the Nine-Hundred Days Memorial in St. Petersburg, Russia. Surrounding the underground memorial, at the top of the walls, are orange lights simulating candles. There are nine-hundred of them, one for each day of the German siege during World War II against the city then known as Leningrad, when millions of her inhabitants died to defend the city against Hitler's Third Reich. You hear music, but not that which is meant to entertain. It is the haunting sounds of a mournful chorus, designed to convey to all the visitors the solemnity of what is being remembered. The rhythm of the music instantly causes you to realize just how terrible it must have been.

When the mighty have fallen, and the nation finds itself in grief, someone has to step to the front and speak for all the people. Who better than David? Those who are real leaders are truly at their best when faced with a crisis. How many times have I had the opportunity to witness people of faith who, when confronted with grief, rise to the highest level of their devotion? You have as well, I'm sure.

If your spiritual journey has spanned the years, think back to those times when strong leaders from your faith tradition have died. Perhaps they had shared the church pew with you. What was your response? You rallied around their families and gave them comfort. You saw your friends stand before the presence of God and the assembled mourners to acknowledge their grief publicly, openly, and with great faith and courage. You witnessed what is without doubt the most hurtful time of life, and yet, you received a newfound strength in God's presence, in God's mercy and grace. Through the witness of your friends, you saw grief and faith interwoven in an inextricable bond, and you knew without doubt that you had been given a great gift — an unwavering witness of true faith.

When the mighty have fallen, political power means nothing. David's words are genuine, and show no political ambition whatsoever. He is not thinking about assuming the throne of Israel. His only concern is with the heart of the people of Israel, and leading them to grieve appropriately. He is providing Israel the time and space to mourn their fallen leader. There will come a time for the government to regroup. There will come that day when tools will be picked up again and the people will go back to work. Soon enough life will settle back down to the daily task of doing what must be done. But now, the only consideration is an appropriate and public grief. With his powerful and poetic words, David gives the people of Israel permission to mourn their dead…for the mighty have fallen.

While it is true that death brings the need for reflection, it is just as true that it also brings a numbness to the soul. It is hard to think, it is hard to hear, it is hard to see. The only thing you can do is feel, and the only thing you feel is a numbing kind of pain. Flannery O'Connor, the famous southern writer of fiction, wrote about characters who seemed to be larger than life. They were always exaggerated in their behavior. She explained why. "To the hard of hearing," she said, "you shout, and for the almost-blind you draw large and startling figures."[2] In other words, this was the only way she knew to get her readers' attention.

David doesn't use fiction. He isn't a prose writer, he's a poet. However, with his stirring lament of Saul and Jonathan, he is getting the attention of the people of Israel, and is leading them in public worship. This just may be David's greatest moment as Israel's leader.

Again, those of you who recall the tragic events surrounding President Kennedy's death in 1963…remember the use of symbolism when our nation buried our fallen leader? There was the long and somber procession through the nation's capital, the caisson and the riderless horse, the seemingly endless line of mourners filing past the casket to give their respect. The salute of young John John before his father's coffin. Our grief was large because our loss was large. We as a nation were hard of hearing and almost blind from grief, so our symbols had to be large and startling to get our attention.

The same is true with David's words:

> *You mountains of Gilboa* (where Saul was slain),
> *let there be no dew or rain upon you,*
> *nor bounteous fields!*
> *For there the shield of the mighty was defiled,*
> *the shield of Saul, anointed with oil no more.*

In David's mind, even the very ground where Saul was slain was to be cursed, just like the Philistines who took his life. The land is to be cursed and unable any more to yield grain. These are large words, meant to symbolize Israel's tremendous loss.

If we are to get a picture in our minds of who the real David was — or make any attempt at all, however misbegotten it might be — under no circumstances can we force our twenty-first century mindset upon these people who lived three thousand years ago. We tend to think of them as sophisticated and urbanized. But they were not. They were primitive nomads, living in tents, roaming from place to place, raiding other villages, living off the land as best they could, utilizing crude tools made of sticks and stones. They were vicious in their dealings with others not of their nationality, and relentless and cruel in forging a place for themselves among their enemies. They were a crude and often unruly people.

Which makes David's words, the sensitivity of his spirit, even that much more extraordinary and all the more remarkable. You would think, with all the technological advances of these last three thousand years — and even more specifically, these last one hundred years — that David would have little or nothing to say to us. In fact, it is generally thought that this body of history, which is a vital part of our scripture, of course, forms some of the oldest written historical accounts known to man. What could this primitive sheepherder-turned-vigilante possibly do or say that would teach us anything?

Well, David can teach us a great deal about how to confront our grief. We tend to camouflage it, put makeup on it, do we not? Or, in our violent society, we tend to cheapen the value of life to the point that taking life means little or nothing, especially if it is portrayed in the movies or on television as "entertainment." But the violence we read about in our newspaper isn't entertainment. It is real, and it is just down the street from where we live. David can teach us that grief is real, and when one person dies, a little bit of all of us dies as well.

David can also teach us that pain isn't the worst thing in life. He can teach us that being hated isn't the worst thing, or being separated from someone you love isn't the worst thing. David can teach us that, while death is real and is cause for genuine lament, even still, it isn't the worst thing. The worst thing in life is being disconnected from God. It is having God's Spirit depart from us.

Perhaps that is what is meant for David to be a man after God's own heart. It means he is connected to the One who is in charge of all this stuff we call *life*. And not even death — the death of Saul and Jonathan — can change that. In fact, when Saul and his sons die on Mount Gilboa, and David is given the news, he is drawn even closer to the One who has anointed his head with oil and caused his cup to run over.

Our connection with God sometimes comes in the form of a bridge between death and life. The difference between David's experience with God and our own is that our bridge is known as Jesus. Our connection with God, through our risen Lord, is the only thing that keeps our lives from becoming fragmented and worthless. It is what gives meaning to the journey, and hope when we are tempted to think that all has been lost. And when grief provides us that connection, it is a gift from God who makes, in eternity — and through Christ — all things new. Even when the mighty have fallen.

Notes

[1]Ben F. Philbeck, Jr., *Broadman Bible Commentary, Volume 3* (Broadman Press: Nashville, Tennessee, 1970), p. 89.

[2]Eugene H. Peterson, *Leap Over a Wall* (HarperCollins: San Francisco, 1997), p. 115.

~ Five ~
The Context of Salvation

"Today I am powerless, even though anointed king; these men, the sons of Zeruiah, are too violent for me" (2 Samuel 3:39).

"Are you able to drink the cup that I drink, or be baptized with the baptism that I am baptized with?" (Mark 10:38).

We had moved our belongings to Florida, having accepted the call to pastor a church on the Gulf Coast. As soon as our furniture was placed in the house we had rented, and before we hardly opened a box, we loaded up our new van and came home to Arkansas for a much-needed two-week vacation before I was to start work. And while we were gone, unknown to us, things started falling apart.

First, a group in the church decided they didn't want one of the staff members to be around anymore, so they got a majority vote of the deacons to have the church ask for his resignation. Then, the outgoing interim pastor, having determined they were wrong — which they were — threatened to write a letter to the congregation encouraging them not to support the deacons — which, as it turned out, they didn't. By the time we returned from our vacation, and before I had even started my work or preached my first sermon, the whole situation had gotten completely out of hand.

When we opened the door to our house, we found a note attached to it which read, "Randy, call me as soon as you get back into town. Bill." Bill was a deacon who had served on the pastor search committee. However, I couldn't call Bill. I didn't have telephone service yet. So, I drove to his house. When he came to the door, without saying "Hello" or "How was your vacation?" he said, "When I tell you what I've got to tell you, you may want to go back to Baltimore."

And that's the way I started my pastorate in Florida. Trust me, it got worse. I would like to say it got worse before it got better, but in almost five years there, it never got any better.

I suppose it could be said that these people behaved as they did in a misguided way of trying to help the church. But it seemed to me that the only thing they were trying to do was build up their own little kingdom in that church.

I wonder if that is the way David might have felt. Saul, the first king of Israel, has died in battle on Mount Gilboa. Immediately, after a reasonable period of mourning has elapsed, political lines are drawn. One of the remaining sons of Saul, Ishbosheth, assumes the throne of Israel, the northern kingdom, and David is anointed the leader of Judah, the southern kingdom. Tribal rivalries become fierce...and bloody. Joab, and his brothers, the sons of Zeruiah, one of David's sisters, are aligned with David, and Abner serves as right-hand man to Ishbosheth. They lead their comrades in skirmishes against one another, and a great deal of blood is shed needlessly. They are of the same people, the people called Hebrews, but not of the same tribes, and right now, when the people of Israel are in political turmoil, tribal loyalty is more important than any other consideration.

Just as David assumes the throne of Judah, just as David is putting his cabinet together and writing his very first state of the union address, just when he is starting to fulfill his God-anointed calling as king after years of running and struggle and loneliness and exile, just when David should be on top of the world, his very own men, led by Joab and the sons of Zeruiah, conspire to make life miserable for him. Maybe they think they are helping Uncle David. Chances are, however, they are simply giving in to their violent instincts. Unfortunately, what they are doing is what they do best, and what they do best is create chaos for all those who are around them. David's political cabinet are a real piece of work.

"David, when I tell you what I've got to tell you, you may want to go back to Bethlehem." David has about as much chance of going back to Bethlehem as we did to Baltimore. It could very well be that Joab and the sons of Zeruiah thought they were helping David, but they weren't. They weren't at all.

Here's the story...

Ishbosheth, the son of Saul and newly-crowned king of Israel, is a weak leader and is really the king in name only. The truth of the matter is that Abner, the commander of the army, is running the show. He is not even very subtle at establishing himself as a king-maker. We are told that it is Abner who makes

Ishbosheth the king. "David grew stronger and stronger," the writer of 2 Samuel says, and all the while "Abner was making himself strong in the house of Saul." He lets it be known to anyone who will listen that "the future is with David,"[1] so his purpose is to persuade the tribes of Israel to align with David and with Judah. Abner is quite the political mover-and-shaker, a real wheeler-dealer.

But Abner has a problem in the person of Joab, David's nephew, the son of Zeruiah. Joab is the kind of young hothead who finds it easier to get forgiveness than permission. "He kills first and then thinks later."[2] Abner and Joab are enemies, one from the northern tribes of Israel and the other from the southern tribe of Judah. In their first battle, which was really supposed to be nothing more than an athletic contest, Abner — though he doesn't want to — slays Joab's brother, Asahel. Asahel pursues him until there is a stand-off. When there is a stand-off, someone has to die. In this case, it is Asahel. Asahel's death sets off a frenzy of violence and before the dust has settled, 360 of Abner's men have died and twenty of Joab's are dead. The bad blood between them grows ever hotter, and Joab swears revenge for the life of his brother Asahel. If you know anything of Shakespeare's play, *Romeo and Juliet*, and the ill-fated skirmishes between the families Capulet and Montague, then you get a picture of what is happening here between the young hotheads of Israel and Judah. Who knows? This story may have been Shakespeare's motivation.

Joab has sworn revenge, and he gets it. When Abner comes to David in peace, with a plan to bring the tribes of Israel into alignment with Judah, Joab takes Abner's life in the same manner as Abner had killed Asahel. "An eye for an eye, and a tooth for a tooth." Or, perhaps to put it more realistically, "do it to them before they have a chance to do it to you." That's the code of Joab, the son of Zeruiah. David immediately pronounces a curse upon Joab's family, even though Joab *is* family.

It is a strange way for God's people to behave, is it not? But remember, as we have said before, these are not urbane and sophisticated people. They are nomadic tribesmen who live by the code of tooth and claw. "Do unto others before they have the opportunity to do it to you." "Lust and deceit. Assassination and murder."[3] It is, unfortunately, a way of life for the people of Israel and Judah.

This is an improvement over the way it was before? We are told that God's Spirit had departed from Saul and that David was a man after God's own heart. Does that include his family and friends? Is this the way God's people are supposed to behave? Does this have anything to do whatsoever with the will and the purposes of God? It sounds far more like an R-rated movie plot than holy scripture. Isn't scripture supposed to portray goodness and light? What's with all this political intrigue? If God is really in charge, why doesn't God simply cut to the chase and take over this situation? Why does God let hotheaded jerks like Abner and Joab play their little, and very dangerous, games?

Well, the only goodness and light you are going to find in the scriptures are in the Garden of Eden before Adam and Eve decided to picnic in forbidden places. After that, *this* is the kind of stuff you will find in scripture because this is the kind of stuff you find in life. It was true in the days of David, and it's just as true now. The Bible doesn't sugarcoat life. In that respect, except for the fact that this was written three thousand years ago, it reads like our daily newspaper. It simply tells it like it is. But the difference between the Bible and your local newspaper is that the Bible also portrays what God's intention is in doing something about it. If the story of Abner and Joab tells us nothing else, it reveals that God has imperfect people to deal with. His love is perfect, and his salvation is likewise, but if it weren't for the Abners and Joabs of the world, would grace and mercy and salvation be necessary?

In other words, this is the context in which God chooses to work out his salvation for his people. David's story, like life, is a mixture of good and bad. For every plotter like Abner, there is an Ahimelech, the priest of Nob who gave David bread when he was hungry and a sword when he was defenseless. For every assassin like Joab, there is a Jonathan, who loved David with all his heart, yet remained loyal to his father Saul. God reaches down into the mix of good and bad, clean and dirty, antiseptic and bloody, and lets us know this is God's world and not just ours. God walks right into the midst of the front pages of life and gives grace and salvation to all who would believe.

And that is true, even when it comes to sending his own Son into this mixed-up world. You see, for every David there is also a Herod. If Jesus was a descendent of David, then Herod was at least cut from the same piece of cloth as Saul, for he too was as crazy as a loon. In the year 7 B.C., when Herod was king of Judah, he feared that his sons were lusting after his throne. So he did the only sensible thing a king should do under the circumstances, right? He had three of his sons assassinated. Five days before his death, he had another son killed. And then, fearing that his own death might cause joy in the land (which I'm sure it did) he left the command that at his death the oldest male child in each home in Judah was to be killed so there would be a guarantee that everyone in the land would be in grief. If they weren't going to grieve over him, at least they would be grieving over somebody. A real sweetheart, that Herod, huh? His command, by the way, was not carried out. Dead men can't wreak vengeance, and he certainly didn't have any sons left to do it for him.

This, of course, is the same Herod who carried out the slaughter of all the male children two years of age or younger when he got word through some traveling magi that a new king had been born in the region of Bethlehem.

This is the kind of world into which Jesus was born. It makes Abner and Joab, and all their political shenanigans, look rather mild, doesn't it? And we would hope that Jesus, through his ministry of healing the sick and feeding the poor and preaching the good news of salvation, would have changed everything; everything for the good. But consider that not even his disciples understood what his mission truly was.

One day, after they had been with him for almost three years (enough time, we would think, for his long-range plan to have been understood by his disciples), the brothers James and John, sons of Zebedee, sidle up next to Jesus as they walk toward Jerusalem. "Master, we have a request of you."

"Oh, what is it, boys?"

"Well, we've been talking, you see, and uh…well, when you come into your kingdom… uh, well…"

"Come on, boys, get to the point. What is it you want?"

"Well, when you come into your kingdom we would like to sit on your right hand and your left hand. Please, please? Can we, please?"

Just call them Abner and Joab. Some things, like political ambition, never change. And just like Abner and Joab thought they were helping David establish his kingdom, James and John no doubt think they are doing the same for Jesus. They are obviously the right men for the job, so having them in these important positions could do nothing but help Jesus in his kingdom efforts, right? And besides, it doesn't hurt to have a little ambition. At least that's what mama says.

Ever heard the adage, "With friends like this, who needs enemies?" You won't find those exact words in the Bible, but you will find plenty of Abners and Joabs and James and Johns to back it up.

In late December, 1995 I stood in England's Canterbury Cathedral at the very spot, in front of the altar, where Thomas Becket, the Archbishop of Canterbury, was murdered by four knights loyal to King Henry II. As the story goes, Becket had been critical of the king. King Henry was overheard by his knights to say, "Not one will deliver me from this low-born priest." And taking him literally, they then took matters into their own hands. It seems there are

Abners and Joabs in every generation.

Deaf and dumb, that's what they were — Abner and Joab, James and John — deaf and dumb to the ways and intentions of God. They had no clue as to what God's purposes were, but they did not let that stand in the way of their charging full-speed ahead into the deep and swirling political waters of their day.

Let's consider the difference in these two stories. Joab remains a thorn in David's side all the days of his life. He is loyal to David, but is self-willed to a fault, with no ethics to boot. David gives up in despair. "Today I am powerless," he says, "even though anointed king; these men, the sons of Zeruiah, are too violent for me." David is attempting to establish a kingdom based on justice and peace. David is trying to re-direct his people to a stronger acknowledgment of their God. And the sons of Zeruiah (of his very own blood!) in their misguided attempts to be of help, prove to be nothing but a problem to the man who is after God's own heart.

Jesus, the descendent of David, in response to the request of James and John, says, *"Are you able to drink the cup that I drink, or be baptized with the baptism that I am baptized with? The cup that I drink you will drink; and with the baptism with which I am baptized, you will be baptized..."* In other words, "The time will come, boys, when you will know the way of my Father's kingdom, and you will follow it. Your political ambitions will no longer matter. You will find yourself doing only the will of the Father."

What is the difference between Abner and Joab and James and John? David threw up his hands in despair. Jesus gave up his hands to be nailed to the cross. The difference is the cross. In fact, the difference in everything is the cross. The world doesn't change from generation to generation, from three thousand years ago to today. Political ambition and intrigue, selfishness and sin: they are always alive and well, regardless of the times. This will always be the context in which God brings about salvation. The difference is the cross.

If it is true of David's time three thousand years ago, if it is true of Jesus' time two thousand years ago, then surely it is just as true of our time as well. Into the midst of our deepest failings comes Jesus to rescue us from our sin. And because of that, somehow we have to keep on believing that God is continuing to work out his eternal purpose even in the moral and political, social and cultural conditions in which you and I wake up every morning. Yes, it is easy to look at all this and be filled with despair. Yes, it is a wonder that God didn't, like David, throw up his hands in despair a long time ago and give up on us. The sons of Zeruiah are still in our midst, and we cannot help but wonder why God bothers to bother anymore.

But the hope of the gospel is that God hasn't given up; for if God has, the cross means nothing. Think of the kind of political trickery that put Jesus there, and then realize that nothing, not even the sons of Zeruiah, can keep God from sharing with us his eternal salvation.

Notes

[1]Eugene H. Peterson, *Leap Over a Wall* (Harper: San Francisco, 1997), p. 126.

[2]Ibid.

[3]Ibid., p. 129.

~ Six ~
A Long Stride and a Large Embrace

"And David became greater and greater, for the Lord, the God of hosts, was with him" (2 Samuel 5:10).

Since our move to Louisville, Kentucky, in 1971 to attend seminary, my wife and I lived in a number of different places before returning to our native state in 1993. In every place we have lived, we sought to find something aesthetically beautiful about our new hometown that would make us proud to live there.

There was Euclid Avenue in Bristol, Virginia. The avenue had old, distinguished homes on both sides with a beautiful tree-lined median dividing the street. The very first time we visited there, we drove down the avenue and knew instinctively that this was the place for us to do our pastoral internship. Two years later we found there was much about Nashville to commend it, but what I liked best were the tree-covered hills surrounding the city and all of middle Tennessee. Having grown up in the flat Delta land of northeast Arkansas, it was a welcome change. In Baltimore some friends in our church had a boat on which we would occasionally cruise the Chesapeake Bay. On Monday holidays we would go down to Annapolis or over to Baltimore's beautiful Inner Harbor. After moving to Florida, we enjoyed the beaches of Florida's Gulf Coast, though I admit our daughter Emily spent more time there than anyone else in the family.

When you are considering moving to a new place, you think of things like this. Apart from the obvious employment opportunities, will we enjoy where we live? Is it the kind of place where we would want our friends and family to come and visit? Will we be proud of our new city?

David, the new king of Israel, is thinking about making a move.

48

Somehow, though, I doubt if the questions we asked came anywhere close to David's consideration when he was making his plans to move from Hebron to Jerusalem. There was certainly nothing aesthetically beautiful about Jerusalem that would make him want to establish his new home there. There were no tree-lined avenues or surrounding hills, no beaches or waterways. Nor was it a large city. That would mean no major league baseball team or professional opera. And besides, it's a certainty the inhabitants will not be friendly. In fact, it's a sure bet they will be downright hostile. No, it appears that David has one reason and one reason alone for wanting to make his new headquarters in the city of the Jebusites. You will find it in the mantra of all realtors: "location, location, location."

David has finally brought together the northern tribes of Israel and the southern tribe of Judah into one nation. After many years of being separated from one another tribally, the people of God called the Hebrews, are finally united under one flag. Rare, but wonderful, are those fleeting moments in life when what has been a future hope becomes a present reality. David is experiencing just such a moment, and surely it is a heady feeling. Finally, finally, he is king over not just Judah but all the twelve tribes of Israel. The very thought of that is enough to make his skin tingle. Imagine it: he is God's anointed, and now he is king over all Israel!

But even in the best of times, there are problems. I was reminded once by a friend that there is no such thing as a problem; it is an opportunity. If that indeed is true, David has a *real* opportunity on his hands. Hebron, where he has established his throne since becoming first the king of Judah, is in the southern kingdom. Now that he is king over all Israel, and not just Judah, if he remains in Hebron it will be quite difficult to keep a watch on the northern tribes. If he moves his headquarters north, he might not be able to control Judah. Not only that, but David has outgrown Hebron. So, David needs to move. The only question is, where?

Walter Wangerin has an interesting perspective on this story.[1] He imagines David lying in his bed thinking about his logistical problems. David's secretary, Seraiah, knows seven languages and writes all of David's correspondence. Seraiah keeps an account of the acts of the king, but there is no room for the records. Jehoshaphat is the king's herald. He handles the affairs of state, but he lives at a distance from David's house. He should be *in* the house, available to David at a moment's notice. Benaiah is David's personal bodyguard and has several troops at his disposal. There isn't enough room to house the secret service. Joab is David's commander-in-chief.

Hebron's citizens are beginning to resist the imperious attitude of the soldiers who sleep in their houses and eat their food. Not only is David's house too small, but so is his city.

As he lies in bed, David looks up at the oakwood beams and the gray clay troweled between them. "Tomorrow," David says to himself, "my ceiling will be cedar. And my house — " David ponders the thought, his hands behind his head, gazing upward, gazing *through* the ceiling, and then he whispers, "My house will be in Jerusalem."

It makes so much sense. He needs a new capital city, "a place all his own, unencumbered by Israel's old memories."[2] And the only logical choice is Jerusalem. Why Jerusalem? Jerusalem sits right on the line between the two kingdoms and has never been claimed by either the north or the south. Jerusalem. It is a perfect choice. Jerusalem. Location, location, location.

There is just one problem, however...er, opportunity. The Jebusites. The Jebusites, who have inhabited Jerusalem for centuries, are a formidable foe and will not easily give up their city to the Hebrews. In fact, they will not give it up at all if they have anything to say about it, and they intend to say plenty about it. David really has his work cut out for him if wants to take the city of the Jebusites.

The Jebusites are also rather cocky. For centuries, raiding armies had attempted to take Jerusalem and none of them had been successful. Even Joshua, in his successful campaign to take the land for the Hebrews in the name of their God Yahweh, left Jerusalem alone and set his sights on Jericho. "You will not come in here," the Jebusites called out to David. "Even the blind and the lame will turn you back." It was their way of saying that they could keep David and his armies from overtaking the city even if they were blindfolded and had one arm tied behind their backs. The Jebusites were cocky, all right, and for good reason. No one had ever been able to take their city, and they were convinced no one ever would. Not even David, the conqueror of the Philistines, the most famous and fearless leader in all the land between the Nile and the Euphrates.

But, the Jebusites had never before reckoned with David, who now is king over all Israel. David, now thirty-seven years old, is in the prime of his life. He has all the momentum on his side. What David wants, David gets. He has developed an insatiable appetite. After all, he has seven wives and six sons. Obviously a sign of God's blessings! If David wants Jerusalem, David gets Jerusalem, as simple as that. And he's not about to let a bunch of arrogant

Jebusites keep him from it. After all, David has not a small dose of self-confidence as well.

It is interesting that David has allowed the ruthless Joab to be the commander-in-chief of his armies. Joab, the eldest son of Zeruiah, David's sister. Joab, who has slain Abner, and has "the tyrant's arrogance and the soldier's impatience."[3] But when it comes to the battle plan for the taking of Jerusalem, look who is in charge. It is not Joab but David who determines how the city will be taken. It is David who knows that every city, every village, every encampment, has at least one weakness that can be exploited, and he shares his plan with Joab. Jerusalem's Achilles' Heel is the water shaft. David tells his officers that the soldiers are to shimmy up the water shaft and take the Jebusites by surprise. Then, they can open the gate of the city from the inside and let the remaining troops enter. "We will see," David says to Joab, "how well the blind and the lame of Jerusalem do then."

And that is how David and his men took Jerusalem that day. For all we know, it could have been a bloodless coup. That's doubtful, however, since Joab was in charge of military operations and Joab was a killer of the first order. Nevertheless, it was an easy victory, and the Jebusites, even those who were not blind or lame, could not keep David from getting what he wanted. And what David wanted was Jerusalem. He was so proud of his new city that he named it "The City of David." It is obvious that God's future for Israel is not only tied up in a young man named David, but in a city as well. From now on, Jerusalem will be not only the city of David, it will be Zion, the city of God.

The writer of 2 Samuel concludes the story of the taking of Jerusalem by saying, "And David became greater and greater, for the Lord, the God of hosts, was with him." *Halok v'gadol* is the Hebrew phrase that is used. It means "greater and greater." It has been suggested that another translation of that phrase could be that David proceeded from that moment on with "a longer stride and a larger embrace."[4]

That's a wonderfully poetic way of putting it, "a longer stride and a larger embrace." But what does it mean? Perhaps it means this: now that David has his own home, his own city from which to govern, now that life really has come together for David, he has the ability to become a man truly after God's own heart. He has the opportunity now to reach his full potential as the one who will lead God's people to fulfill God's purposes and intentions. David has an open road in front of him, and it's full-speed ahead.

Up to this point, his life has been lived on the margin. He has had to live defensively because of his great enemy, Saul. He has had to endure the machinations of those around him, like the sons of Zeruiah, who think they are helping him but are really making life difficult for him. The fulfillment of his greatest dreams had been just that: dreams. But now, he is king over Israel. He has his own city from which to govern his people. He is a man after God's own heart. David now has a longer stride and a larger embrace.

With a long stride comes a large shadow. A large shadow means influence and power. With a large embrace comes the ability to reach out to people, especially people who are in need of the kind of leadership Saul was simply unable to give them. David is now faced with the perfect opportunity (and it is not disguised as a problem) to bring abundance and joy and peace to the people of Israel, and to do it in the name of the God who has called them together as a people. It is perhaps the greatest time in all of Israel's history. It is truly the golden age, not only for David, but for his people as well.

"A longer stride and a larger embrace." It is also a reminder that David isn't *David* apart from God.[5] What David has become is due to God's blessings upon him, and this is a time in David's life when he acknowledges that as a spiritual reality. There will be times when he loses sight of it, but right now — right now — he is more aware of it than anyone. He would not be who he is, and certainly would not be where he is, were it not for God's divine guidance and intervention.

Who of us cannot say the same? The sooner you and I realize that the same is true for ourselves, the sooner we too will have a longer stride and a larger embrace. We may never claim a city for ourselves, or certainly have one named for us, but that doesn't mean our stride can't be longer and our embrace larger. There is nothing to keep us from casting a larger shadow and having a wide enough embrace that all are included within it.

So how do we do it? How do we have this longer stride and larger embrace?

To answer that, let's not stop with David. Let's move on to consider David's descendent named Jesus. David conquered Jerusalem, and a thousand years later Jesus wept over Jerusalem, over her unwillingness to carry out the purposes of God. In his Sermon on the Mount, Jesus did not plot how best to overcome the enemy, he encouraged his followers to love their enemies. In fact, he went so far as to say that to love one's enemy or one's neighbor was the same as loving God. Then, after saying this, which is a hard enough thing to swallow, he said, *"Be perfect, therefore, as your heavenly Father is perfect."*

We have a hard time with that one, don't we? And because of it, Jesus' words cannot be interpreted without backing down from them a bit. It has always been interesting to me that those who talk so much about taking the Bible literally are more than willing to take Jesus' words in the Sermon on the Mount figuratively. That is especially true here. How can we possibly be perfect like God? So, we back down from Jesus' words, do we not?

We know — we *all* know — that we can't be perfect, certainly as God is perfect. What's more, Jesus surely knew it too. So what does he mean? Consider it this way: we are to let our stride be longer and our embrace larger. We are to live generously toward others, especially those who are unlike ourselves. We are to be gracious toward others, especially toward those who are less than gracious toward us. In other words, we are to try and relate to others as God has made it evident God relates toward us.

Do you see what has happened? We have backed off Jesus' difficult words, and then as we have attempted once more to define and interpret them — to "repackage" them so they will be more acceptable to us — they moved us right back to what Jesus was talking about. You cannot take Jesus seriously and back down from what he tells you. The only way to love others is to do it as God loves us. The only way to be gracious to others is to mirror God's grace toward us. The only way to give is as God gives to us. The only way to understand others is as God is understanding toward us. We are to be like God! We are to have a longer stride and a larger embrace.

We have come to the point in David's life when he is at his absolute best. He establishes justice among his people and, as much as possible, brings peace and security to the land. He encourages his people, once again, to participate in a consistent worship of God. At no other time in David's life is he more a man after God's own heart.

Can the same be said of you and me? Have you been thinking lately of making a move? It doesn't require a change of address on our part for us to have God's heart. But it does call for a willingness to journey in God's direction, to let God lead us to be at our best. May our stride be long and our embrace large because we too are after God's own heart.

Notes

[1]Walter Wangerin, *The Book of God: The Bible as a Novel* (Zondervan: Grand Rapids, Michigan, 1996), pp. 309-310.

[2]Walter Brueggemann, *Interpretation: First and Second Samuel* (John Knox Press: Louisville, Kentucky, 1990), p. 239.

[3]Wangerin, p. 309.

[4]Eugene H. Peterson, *Leap Over a Wall* (Harper: San Francisco, 1997), p. 135.

[5]Peterson, p. 138.

~ Seven ~
God in a Box

"David was afraid of the Lord that day..." (2 Samuel 6:1-9).

Counting the churches I pastored while a student in college and seminary, I have shepherded eight different congregations in five different states. So I think I can say with some authority, based on my experience in these various places, that there is a certain dynamic involved when a new pastor comes on the field. This is not exactly earthshaking news. In fact, it is quite obvious.

When a new person comes to lead a church, there is a wonderful sense of excitement on the part of the congregation and the new pastor. The slate is absolutely clean. No mistakes have yet been made by either side. Everyone knows that mistakes will occur, but at that given moment, there is a state of "wedded bliss," which is why the early portion of one's pastorate is referred to as "the honeymoon."

However, and this may not be so obvious, there is also a certain degree of wariness as well; a tendency, especially on the part of the congregation, to have a wait-and-see attitude. During this time the new pastor is somewhat on trial. I say "somewhat" because, at the same time they are watching the new pastor with some scrutiny, the people also want to get to know the pastor, help him or her in this new ecclesiastical environment, see that she or he gets off on the right foot. Both sides are attempting to gain the support of the other while holding back a bit to see just how this new relationship is going to work out; all the while hoping and praying it will be a good one, and will last for a long, long time.

Another dynamic involved in this situation is that the new pastor brings his or her own unique gifts and perspectives to the church, none of which the congregation has ever witnessed before. Fresh ideas will be generated, concepts that will spark an enthusiastic response. And even if the immediate reaction is less than positive, most folk are willing to give the new kid on the block a certain amount of leeway. Who knows, this just might be a good thing that is being proposed after all. We've never done it that way before, but let's wait and see. Let's wait and see; cut her some slack, give him some rope.

If the new pastor has any wisdom at all, however, he will not barge in right away, attempting to change things and do that which will immediately create problems for himself and his parishioners. She will listen more than she will talk. He will learn where the people are in their attitudes and feelings, and in doing so get a sense of the church's past. She will discover where the church has been and whether certain elements of the church's past need to be brought into the present reality. Sometimes, that which has been significant to the church years before has become lost along the way and needs to be resurrected — or at least dusted off — given new life, and brought before the people again.

I can give you an example from my own experience in my current church. Somehow, in the time before I came, there was a sense among the congregation that under the previous pastoral leadership the church's allegiance to traditional worship had been…well, violated. They wanted a return to the way worship was done before. I know that to be true because they told me so very directly, and because they called me to be their pastor knowing that traditional worship is my preference as well. Our common affirmation of this form of worship has, for the most part, been the reason why these years have found us getting along so well together. When friends ask me how things are going with my church, I gladly tell them I've been there since 1996 and we're still honeymooning!

Well, the same dynamics which exist between a church and her new pastor were largely the same for David, the new king of Israel, and the reunited kingdom for which he is largely responsible. He is still, in the account recorded in 2 Samuel 6, the new kid on the block. He has made the bold move from Hebron to Jerusalem (talk about change!), establishing the city of the Jebusites as the new capital of the freshly united Israel. He has been successful in bringing the northern and southern kingdoms together, at least politically. But being aligned politically doesn't mean the people are on the same page spiritually, to say the least. David needs a plan — a bold, courageous plan — one that will unite the hearts of the Hebrews and will blend together the traditions of the old tribal way of life and the challenges of this new alliance built on the royalty of a kingship. To put it more piously, David needs to bring his people back to God. What will do it? What will David's plan be?

It is also possible to look upon David's situation from another perspective. It could very well be that David is getting just a little bit cocky. He is on a roll, has the momentum going for him, and wants to keep it that way. So he figures the best way to do that is to do something dramatic and bold. And isn't it true that once you do something out of the ordinary, you find yourself wanting to do something even more extraordinary? An athlete who breaks a record is never satisfied but to break even that record. It goes with the territory of being a leader. It also has to do with momentum.

Momentum is a powerful thing. Do you remember Don Meredith who used to provide the commentary on ABC's *Monday Night Football*? Perhaps as no one else ever has, he brought the issue of momentum to our awareness. When the flow of the game would shift from one team to another, "Dandy Don" would say, "Old 'Mo' has changed jerseys."

Well, David has the momentum. He's wearing the jersey. He's setting new records and is on a roll. Nothing is stopping him. What David wants, David gets. He has an insatiable appetite and finds himself at a point in life in which very little is being denied him. "Strike while the iron is hot," they always say, and David is about to do just that. Suddenly, he remembers the ark of the covenant and recalls what it symbolizes for his people.

The ark of the covenant was quite possibly made by Moses himself. It was basically just a wooden chest which contained relics important to the religious life of Israel, not the least of which were the Ten Commandment tablets brought down from Mount Sinai by Moses. Other items in the ark were a jar of manna, to remind the Israelites of God's provisions for them during their wilderness wanderings, and the rod used by Aaron, the brother of Moses, a reminder of God's salvation. Later, an elaborate top was made of gold, giving added significance to what it represented to the Hebrew people. The ark was considered by the Hebrews as the extension, or even the embodiment, of Yahweh God. It had been taken from the Israelites by the Philistines in battle, but when the plague came to the Philistines, they considered the ark to be bad luck. So, they returned it. It had been stored for some twenty years in the home of a man named Abinadab, the priest of Kiriath-jearim.

For David, and the people of Israel, the symbol of the nation and their collective faith in the one true God, has to be something very tangible, something that will capture the imagination and excitement of the people. After all, kings have to have big ideas, and this one has to be the biggest of them all. What will it be? Suddenly, an inspiration, come down from heaven itself, bursts upon David's mind and heart like a lightning bolt. The ark of the covenant! David will retrieve the ark of the covenant! The ark will represent the newly-rediscovered unity of Israel under David's leadership. Yes indeed, the ark needs to come home.

David decides the ark should be in Jerusalem, where it would take its rightful place among the people of God. Perhaps there is the element of self-serving in this idea as well. The ark of the covenant would be the perfect symbol of David's destiny as king of Israel. Not only will he be king over all Israel, he will establish a royal and religious throne. He will bring God and God's people together in a way not seen since the days of Moses. The ark's presence in Jerusalem will solidify this in the minds and hearts of his people. Nothing will stop him now. "Old Mo" is wearing David's jersey.

I am of the Baptist tradition. Historically, we Baptists have not put a lot of stock in religious relics. But even we know that such venerated objects can at times take on a certain power of their own. As I write these words, my wife and I are sequestered on the tiny western Scottish island of Iona, in the Inner Hebrides. However, my thoughts are on central Scotland; more specifically Bannockburn, the lofty brae overlooking the royal city of Stirling upon which Sir Robert the Bruce, King of the Scots, encountered the English forces of Edward II in 1314. Riding the wave of momentum established by his late colleague William "Braveheart" Wallace, it is said that Robert's forces were emboldened by the presence of the Monymusk Reliquary, an ornate eighth-century cask, which contained the relics of St. Columba, the founder of Christianity in Scotland. Sometimes, relics are very important indeed.

No less was true of the ark of the covenant. There were specific rules about how it was to be transported. Poles were to be placed through the handles on the side. No human hands were to touch it. To do so meant immediate death. Somewhere, somehow, somebody forgot the rules. Instead of having the ark transported from Kiriath-jearim to Jerusalem by having the priests carry it on their shoulders by means of the attached poles, David had a new cart made for the journey. Along the way, one of the oxen leading the cart stumbled in a rut. The ark listed to one side and appeared to fall off the cart onto the ground. One of the sons of Abinadab, whose name was Uzzah, instinctively reached up to keep the ark from falling. And when he did, he fell dead.

There is no indication that he died of fright when he realized that what he had done was against the rules of God. The writer of 2 Samuel interprets it this way: "The anger of the Lord was kindled against Uzzah; and God struck him there because he reached out his hand to the ark."

Now get the picture clearly in your mind, if you will. David has made a big production of this. He's gathered thousands of his people and turned this into a real processional. They're singing and dancing in front of the ark, they've brought along their harps and lyres and tambourines and castanets and cymbals. If they'd had bass drums and fiddles — or bagpipes! — they would have brought them too. This is the Macy's Parade and the Rose Bowl Parade both rolled into one. But as they make their journey to Jerusalem, the ox slips, the ark begins to slide from the cart, Uzzah reaches out to steady it, and he falls dead on the ground. The music stops, the people stare in disbelief, and David begins shaking like a leaf.

"David was afraid of God that day," the narrator says. Who wouldn't be? But David was also angry; so angry he called the whole thing off. "Everybody go home," he said, "the party's over." The closest house belonged to a Philistine named Obed-edom. They took the ark to his house and stored it in the garage, and David sulked all the way back to Jerusalem. He had them put it in the house of a Philistine, for crying out loud! *That's* how upset David was!

It is the first time since becoming king of Israel that David doesn't get his way. David has become accustomed to getting what he wanted. He has wanted the ark in Jerusalem. It would have been so perfect! It seemed like such a good plan. Why would God do such a thing, just because Uzzah tried to do the right thing and keep the ark from falling on the ground. What kind of God is this?

It is, admittedly, one of the most difficult passages in all of scripture to understand and interpret redemptively. We don't understand how or why God would strike someone dead, especially someone who is in his service as a priest. Of course, we could say that this is the interpretation of the story writer, and he could be wrong. We could say that, but that leaves us with a bit of a bad taste in our mouths, does it not? Besides, we are told by Luke a thousand years later, in the Book of Acts, that God does it again, this time to Ananias and Sapphira when they are less than honest about their offering to the church. Are you bothered by this? I confess quite honestly that I am. We look to scripture for help in understanding this, and there appears to be none. Let's face it: there are times in scripture when God seems to act not like the God we want our God to be.

Not only that, but scripture can be unfair at times; or worse, scripture does not play by our rules of fairness. We are told what happens, and by whom, but not always does the Bible tell us *why* something happens. That is true here. Uzzah dies when he reaches over to steady the ark; that we know. And according to the narrator who states it quite bluntly, God kills him, out of anger no less. That we know. But we aren't told why.

And God evidently doesn't bother to let David in on it, either. If we are puzzled by this, imagine how David must have felt. He gets mad as a hornet at God. If God didn't want anybody to touch the ark, why didn't God tell David not to have the cart made? Why didn't God go over the rules again with David, or why didn't God just tell David to leave the ark right where it was so it couldn't hurt anybody? Is there anybody here who can blame David for calling off the parade and sending everybody home? Just when the people of Israel are given the opportunity to celebrate their newfound relationship with one another and with God, this happens. What begins as a wonderful blessing for David and his people turns out to be a curse. It just doesn't make any sense.

People have tried to explain why God would do such a thing. In fact, the New International Version of the Bible interprets verse seven as saying that "the Lord's anger burned against Uzzah *because of his irreverent act.*" Personally, I think that's a bit of a stretch. We are not told that what Uzzah did was irreverent. That's an interpretation, not a translation.

But we cannot deny that this story leaves a big gap between what happened and why. This narrative from the life of David is just begging us to fill in the blanks, isn't it? Let's give it a try, shall we?

If what Uzzah did that day in touching the ark was not irreverent, it may have at least represented a casual attitude on his part toward God. The ark evidently "possesses great holiness and power."[1] And for that reason, it may not be treated casually, just as the God it symbolizes may not be treated in such a way. After all, the ark has been sitting in the house of Abinadab for twenty years now. Uzzah sees it every day. He becomes familiar with it. When something is there that long, you tend to take it for granted. And you tend to think it belongs to you. Could it be that Uzzah feels some personal ownership of the ark, and therefore it is his responsibility to take care of it? Could it be that to Uzzah, God is in the ark? Could it be that Uzzah, in his own mind and heart, has God in a box?[2] And because Uzzah has God in a box, he is God's custodian? By reaching out to steady the ark, Uzzah is taking care of God?

It is a subtle, but very real temptation, to think one can take care of God. In fact, that seems to be the favorite activity of many well-meaning people today. In attempting to speak for God, when people say they have God's ear and God's tongue exclusively, it is their way of taking care of God. It seems to be the favorite activity of many Christians today. Eugene Peterson puts it this way…

> We enter a church or school to learn God, be trained in knowledge and obedience and prayer. And we get what we came for — truth that centers, words that command and comfort, rituals that stabilize, work that has purpose, a community of relationships that strengthen, forgiveness that frees. We find God. We change our ways. We repent and believe and follow. We rearrange our circumstances and reestablish our routines around what now gives meaning and hope. We take on responsibilities in the wonderful new world of worship and work. We advance in the ranks, and before we know it we're telling others what to do and how to do it. All this is good and right. And then we cross a line — we get bossy and cranky on behalf of God…We take over God's work for him and take charge of making sure others live rightly and well. We get the idea that we're important, self-important, because we're around the Important.[3]

He's right, isn't he? We get comfortable with God and casual in our relationship with God. There's a certain coziness that runs parallel to our feelings of satisfaction that we've got the answers — maybe all the answers — and before we know it we've taken on the idea that we are doing God's work for God. We are God's managers. We develop creeds, even when we deny they are creeds, and if others don't follow them, we tell them they cannot have fellowship with us, for they are not like us. We yield to the temptation that we are God's custodians, and in the process, without our even knowing it, the freedom and joy, the spirit of awe and reverence we once had toward God has shriveled into a lifeless form because we have reduced God to our limited specifications. We've got God in a box.

We know the outcome of this story. David, three months later, is successful in bringing the ark to Jerusalem. And this time the celebration is even greater than the first time around. The people are delighted beyond all measure that God has come to dwell with them. Yet, follow the story through the ensuing years, and you will find that once again the people of Israel begin taking their relationship with God for granted. The ark is in their possession, the one true God is their God, and as long as the ark is with them, so is their God. Yes indeed, they've got God in a box.

Centuries later, the prophets would warn them of the consequences of such narrow thinking. The penalty is exile, which, to the Hebrews, is itself a form of death. When they are forced to leave their native land at the end of the enemy's spear, God remains in Jerusalem and does not cross with them into Babylon. God lives in a particular space, a place that does not include the land of the Babylonians.

> By the rivers of Babylon –
> there we sat down and there we wept
> when we remembered Zion.
> On the willows there we hung up our harps.
> For there our captors asked us for songs
> and our tormentors asked for mirth saying,
> "Sing us one of the songs of Zion!"
>
> How could we sing the Lord's song in a foreign land?
> If I forget you, O Jerusalem,
> let my right hand wither!
> Let my tongue cling to the roof of my mouth,
> if I do not remember you,
> if I do not set Jerusalem above my highest joy (Psalm 137:1-6).

A thousand years after David brings the ark to Jerusalem Jesus comes on the scene. He presents to his people a whole new understanding of God. It is fresh and exciting and people put their faith in him and in the God he has come to proclaim and embody. The ark is no longer needed. And what happens? We divide ourselves into various groups based on our different beliefs, and those who agree with us are right, and in our minds, perhaps even subtly, the others are wrong. We've got God in a box all over again.

God is bigger than anything you and I can ever imagine in a thousand lifetimes. Do you believe that? Do you really? Then don't reduce God to your limited specifications. Don't take God for granted. Don't allow your relationship to God in Christ to become so casual that you think you are his manager. Instead, be ever open to the ways God comes to you and know that you don't take care of God. God will take care of you.

Notes

[1] Bruce Birch, *The New Interpreter's Bible, Volume II* (Abingdon Press: Nashville, 1998) p. 1249).

[2] Eugene H. Peterson, *Leap Over a Wall* (Harper: San Francisco, 1997) p. 150.

[3] Peterson, Ibid., pp. 150-151.

~ Eight ~
When God Says No

"When your days are fulfilled and you lie down with your ancestors, I will raise up your offspring after you, who shall come forth from your body, and I will establish his kingdom" (2 Samuel 7:1-12).

There's nothing more exciting than building a house. My wife and I never had any intention of doing so, but when we moved to Baltimore in 1982 the housing situation was rather tough. People were hanging on to their homes. Mortgage rates were astronomically high. We looked and looked and looked, to no avail. Fortunately, a homebuilder was on our pastor search committee. His son, who was a local realtor, found us a lot in a nice community and three months after we broke ground, we moved in. Our contractor consulted us on all the materials and picked them out himself. He was very kind and generous toward us, and it was a most exciting and pleasant experience.

There's nothing more frustrating than building a house. Several years later, when we moved to Florida, once again we found it difficult to locate a house that we felt suited our needs. We had done it once, why couldn't we do it again? So, we decided to build. Our first builder went bankrupt before we even started (fortunately, after pocketing only $1,000 of our money). Once we located another builder, it took much, much longer than we anticipated, and the subcontractors were completely unreliable. We vowed never to do it again.

There's nothing more frightening than building a house. When you build a house, or do a major renovation for that matter (which we have also done), you better plan to spend a great deal more time and money than you had anticipated. It simply comes with the territory. I don't know about you, but spending that kind of money is genuinely frightening to me.

There's nothing more exciting or frustrating or frightening than building a house.

So, it makes me wonder if David felt any of these emotions when he built his mansion in Jerusalem. My guess is, that being king of Israel, the process goes pretty much as he planned. After all, he has everyone at his beck-and-call. There isn't a person in Jerusalem, except for the Jebusites, I would imagine, who doesn't want to be David's friend. He has neighboring kings giving him building materials, and it's for certain labor is cheap, so he doesn't have to worry about cost overruns. Just about everything is going as he planned. Life is good, and as we have mentioned to you before, David is on a roll. Building a house? Piece o' cake!

The construction of his house is completed and David has all his staff positions filled. His empire is coming along very nicely, and according to the account in 2 Samuel, "The Lord had given him rest from all his enemies around him."

Have you ever gone to bed, or settled into your favorite recliner, finding yourself completely exhausted from the rigors of your day? You craved rest more than anything else in all the world? Perhaps David felt that way, and finally, "The Lord had given him rest from all his enemies around him." David has withstood the vengeful insanity of Saul, endured the needless deaths of his friends and allies, reunited the divided kingdoms of Israel and Judah, moved his capital to Jerusalem, returned the ark of the covenant to the newly-named "City of David," and built himself a luxurious palace suitable for a king of his stature. Whew! David could use a rest, and that is exactly what the Lord gives him.

Or have you ever anticipated a vacation, gotten to your destination, and didn't know what to do with yourself? You just sat there and twiddled your thumbs? I can just picture David sitting on his throne, drumming his fingers, and asking, "What can I do next? What can I do next?" Does it appear to you that David is a Type-A personality? Or maybe he had a slight case of ADD?

Perhaps one star-filled night, David takes a stroll along Mount Moriah. He looks over Jerusalem with her lights twinkling against the darkness and reflects upon what he has built…correction, on what he and God together have built. The lights of the city wink back at the stars in the sky, and David notes that the brightest lights are those which illuminate his wonderful mansion, a mansion constructed from the finest stones and walled with cedar paneling from the mighty forests of Lebanon. And as with all of David's visions — which seemed to be coming these days with lightning speed and great abundance — he realizes what his next major project will be. He has the finest house in Jerusalem, a mansion fit for a king. But God, the One who has made all this possible, still dwells in a tent. It is time to build a house for God.

I get the impression that David is a big-idea kind of guy. He goes from one major project to another. Thinking and dreaming and doing large-scale projects are what keeps his blood pumping and provides him the excitement he needs. If he didn't have his ideas and projects, his life would be unfulfilled. Remember, the writer of this story tells us that the Lord gave David rest from his enemies, but David isn't the kind of person to sit in his recliner for long. He is definitely no couch potato. He needs something to do. Action is rest to David. So he comes up with another big idea. The temple. He will build a house for God. Oh, it will be glorious. He dwells in a house of cedar, but God will dwell in a house of gold!

And God says, "Thanks, but no thanks. If it's all the same to you, I'd prefer to keep things just as they are."

David has shared his grand idea with Nathan, his spiritual adviser. At first, Nathan comes across more like a servant to the king than a prophet of God. "Sure, David. Go ahead and do what you want. You know the Lord gives you your heart's desire." But that very night, God comes to Nathan and says to him, "Don't presume to speak so quickly for me the next time David shares one of his ideas with you. Just because David has an idea doesn't mean I will automatically endorse it. No, you go and tell David that I don't need a house because I have never been confined to a building and I don't intend to start now."

And then God gets really personal. "You go and remind David that it was I who took him out of the pasture where he was tending sheep. It was I who anointed him a prince over Israel, even though he was a nobody, merely the eighth son of an obscure man named Jesse from an insignificant village called Bethlehem. It is I who have been with him wherever he has gone. It is I who gave his enemies into his hands. It is I who am in charge of the program around here. I don't mind David's ideas, but I have veto power, and in this case I'm going to use it. Tell David the answer is 'no'!"

I have a feeling Nathan didn't relish the idea of relaying God's message to David. With royalty comes the expectation that whatever the king wants, the king gets. There aren't very many people still alive in the land who are willing to tell David no, and Nathan isn't excited about being the Lone Ranger on this one. As Nathan tells his king what God has said, David's eyes squint into narrow slits and his mouth becomes hard. This isn't the response he was looking for, and he isn't at all happy about it. Not one bit.

But David learned a lesson that day that you and I would be well advised to understand. When God says no, God means no. Scripture also provides us another insight. When God says no, God's no is always better than our yes, and God also provides a promise. God's promise is that his answer is better than the one we are looking for. It may not seem like it at the time, but it is true. That is exactly what happened in this case. God said no but made David a promise in return, a promise that yielded far greater, and more eternal, consequences than David could ever imagine. In doing this, God provided a word play that is helpful to our understanding of this story.

No, David may not build God a house, but God will build David a house. Wait a minute, let's get this straight now. God is going to build David a house? Why? David has just finished a building project. Why, he's got twenty bedrooms and thirty bathrooms (and he's going to need them, considering all his wives and lady friends). He has a library that would make Congress envious and a war room complete with the latest technology. He has his own gymnasium where he can keep his body toned, and a sauna and whirlpool where he can relax late at night. There's even a huge playground where his many children can go and not be underfoot all day. David has the most luxurious house in all the land. What is this talk about God building David a house? Can God provide him a house that would be an improvement over what he already has?

It's a good question, and here's the answer: when God says he will build David a house, he doesn't mean one made of brick and mortar, or even gold and cedar. God is promising David a royal dynasty. "When your days are fulfilled and you lie down with your ancestors, I will raise up your offspring after you, who shall come forth from your body, and I will establish his kingdom. No matter how sinful your children may be," God is saying to David, "I will not remove my steadfast love from those who come from David's loins." God had withdrawn his blessing from Saul, but he is promising David it will never happen to him or his descendants.

And it is precisely as a fulfillment of that promise that one thousand years later Jesus, a direct descendant of David, came into the world. You see, Solomon, David's son, followed in the royal lineage and ruled Israel for many years. Solomon had great promise and, as we know, great wisdom, but to say that things turned sour near the end is an understatement. Solomon's son Rehoboam proved to be even worse. He was an evil dictator who made life miserable for the Israelites. The elders, who had advised his father, suggested he go easy on the people, but Rehoboam listened to his hotheaded peers instead. He said to the people, "My little finger is thicker than my father's loins. Whereas my father laid on you a heavy yoke, I will add to your yoke. My father disciplined you with whips, but I will discipline you with scorpions." It only got worse after that, and eventually the tribes of Israel found themselves engaged in civil war, largely because of wicked and ineffective leadership from their kings, kings who were David's descendants. Years later they were taken by the Babylonians into exile, and David's dynasty was broken and dissolved. Does that mean God's promise was broken?

Well, consider this…In their gospels, both Matthew and Luke go to great pains to reveal Jesus of Nazareth as a direct descendant of David. Jesus is the great and final fulfillment of all that God had promised David that day through Nathan. And when the religious leadership of Jerusalem rejected Jesus, and it became obvious that he would be put on a Roman cross, he asked that God would remove this "cup," as he called it, this tremendous burden, from him. And God said what? God said no, just as he had done with David years before. God said no. Actually, God didn't say anything, but when God doesn't say anything, God's answer is no. But when God says no, remember, God gives us a promise, a promise that is better than our yes. God lets us in on what are God's hopes and dreams and plans.

Has God ever told you no? In the spring of 1986, we were talking with two pastor search committees. One church was in Florida and the other was the First Baptist Church in a small town in Virginia not far from Washington, D.C. I knew the church in Virginia was more compatible with my style of ministry, and my inclination was to say yes to their invitation to come and be their pastor. But after much prayer and careful consideration I chose the church in Florida. As I have recounted for you before, the situation in Florida was a disaster from the very beginning. Hindsight tells me I should have taken the church in Virginia. Our daughter was only a year from high school, and the town had a privately-endowed public high school which afforded a wonderful education for its youth. The church had a reputation for keeping its pastors a long, long time. In fact, there is a possibility that had we gone there, we might still be there. We would have saved ourselves from the difficulties the next five years would bring. But, our lives would be completely different from the way they are now. And we wouldn't be where we are now.

I can't help but wonder if God led us down a certain path from what we really wanted, so we could travel in the direction God wanted. When God says no, God's no is better than our yes, and always comes with a promise.

I would encourage you, as a spiritual exercise, to examine your own life journey. My guess is that you can remember those times when you wanted something — perhaps, as was true of David, even something for God — and you didn't get it. There was a measure of disappointment. You might have even struggled through some bitterness because of it. If that is true, I would encourage you next to consider the bigger picture of your life and think of what God has in store, not only for you but for God's world.

The next time God says no, consider that God's no is better than your yes. And then wait for the promise. It will come. It will come. And it will be better than anything you might have imagined.

~ Nine ~
Justice and Equity

"Is there anyone remaining of the house of Saul to whom I may show the kindness of God?" (2 Samuel 8:3).

My wife Janet can tell you a great deal more about this than I can (she's the real history buff in the family, especially when it comes to romance history), but the chronicles of the British monarchs has been quite bloody. Take King Henry VIII, for example. If he decided he needed to change wives, and couldn't convince the religious authorities of the efficacy of doing so, he simply trumped up some crime against his wife and had her beheaded or divorced.

Did I mention divorce? That required a new church, but when one is king, one can even cause an ecclesiastical split, if need be. Despite the wishes of the pope, the king can issue a royal decree and get the job done. So what if people lose their heads along the way? Whatever the king wants, the king gets...if you are Henry VIII. That may be one reason why it is quite permissible for tourists to literally walk all over his grave in Windsor Castle's cathedral, which, I have to tell you, I did rather gleefully in 1995.

But the bloodletting didn't just have to do with spousal abuse. If the monarchy was being transferred from one family to another, and you were of the family being deposed, you could pretty much count on your life not being worth very much. Because they posed a threat to the new monarchy, it could be expected that all remaining family members would be disposed of, from the oldest to the youngest.

The British have not had a monopoly on this kind of conduct, of course. You will find the same behavior operative in the ancient days of the Egyptians and Romans, and more lately the Russian czars. And, I am sure, the same thing was true in a number of other nations as well. It certainly happened that way in the time of David, king of Israel.

Allow me to retrace our steps in regard to David's life story, in the hope that it will put this account from 2 Samuel in perspective. Jonathan, the son of King Saul, was David's friend. He was caught up in the middle of his father's demented hatred of David, and David's need to defend himself against Saul's insane attempts to take his life. Jonathan managed to remain loyal to his father and yet at the same time maintained his deep, deep friendship with David. It was not an easy thing to do. The writer of these chronicles makes it clear that Jonathan was able to do so out of his great love for David and his intense loyalty toward his father. In other words, Jonathan must have been quite a remarkable young man to have been able to do that.

Saul and his son Jonathan, along with two others of his sons, died together on Mount Gilboa while fighting the hated Philistines. It was a terrible day for the nation of Israel. Their leaders had fallen in battle and it would be certain, as is often true of war, the Philistines would rampage throughout the land pillaging and murdering. No one was safe, but that was especially true of the house of Saul. They would be particular targets of the Philistines and their bloody rage.

Mephibosheth, the son of Jonathan, was five years old when his father died in battle. Word soon arrived at their home in Gibeon as to what had happened in Gilboa, and "panic was immediate and total."[1] It was a foregone conclusion that the Philistines would burn the house and everything, and anyone, in it. "Mercy" was not in the Philistines' vocabulary, especially toward their enemies. Knowing this, Saul's servants quickly grabbed anything they could get their hands on, as if the house were on fire, and ran for their lives. Five-year-old Mephibosheth was carried out by his nurse, but in her haste she dropped him and both of his ankles were broken, rendering him permanently crippled.

Mephibosheth manages to get by for a number of years, living quietly and obscurely in the small village of Lo-debar. He was the only living relative and heir of the once-great house of King Saul, but for the sake of survival it was best to keep his royal identity and his location a secret. After all, there is no statute of limitations on vengeance. Who knows who might still want to take his life, if for no other reason than to insure that the house of Saul would not rise to prominence yet again.

Let's move the scene forward a number of years. David has now been king of Israel for quite some time. He has established Jerusalem as the center of his political leadership. He has constructed a wonderful mansion for himself and his large and extended family, and brought the ark of the covenant to

Jerusalem to symbolize the presence and blessing of Yahweh God. God has given him rest from his enemies, at least for awhile. He is served capably by a large staff who carry out his orders. Life is good for David and for his people. As the writer of 2 Samuel tells us, "So David reigned over all Israel, and David administered justice and equity to all his people." He is a good king and his kingdom is thriving. David's heart is in the right place.

To prove it, one day he asks his advisers, "Is there still anyone left of the house of Saul to whom I may show kindness for Jonathan's sake?" After all these years, his fond memories of Jonathan are still glowing brightly. He reflects on those bittersweet times when he and Jonathan enjoyed hunting together or roaming the Judean hills. Though Saul did everything he could to pull them apart, because of his intense hatred and jealousy of David, their friendship grew stronger each day. David thinks back and gives thanks for the memories that still linger in his mind and heart, memories that reflect difficult, but still wonderful, times.

You would think, if he and Jonathan were that close, that David would have known Mephibosheth, Jonathan's young son. Mephibosheth. Mephibosheth. What ever happened to Mephibosheth? In all these years, with the concerns of leading his people and the demands that such political leadership required of him, do you think David has forgotten Mephibosheth? Evidently not. How old would he be now? Twenty-five, perhaps. Where would he be…if, that is, he were still alive? Could it be possible that Mephibosheth is still alive? So David asks his advisers, "Is there still anyone left of the house of Saul to whom I may show kindness for Jonathan's sake?"

Yes, there is, but it's going to take a little work to sort it all out. David's staff locate a man who had once been one of Saul's servants. His name is Ziba. He is brought before David, and the question is put to him. But notice it takes on a different form when put to Saul's servant. Now David asks, "Is there still anyone remaining of the house of Saul to whom I may show (not kindness for Jonathan's sake but…) *the kindness of God*?" It has turned from being merely a personal mission on David's part to a holy mission. He now wants to be of service to God.

It may very well be the closest that David has ever come, or ever will come, to the personal understanding that to love one's neighbor is the same as loving God. Other than the prophets, it is as close to the gospel of Jesus Christ as can be found, at least this early in the Old Testament. It is, of course, a truth that will come to the light in David's offspring Jesus some one thousand years later. "Is there still anyone remaining of the house of Saul to whom I may show *the kindness of God?*"

And Ziba says, "Yes, the crippled son of Jonathan is still alive."

If David had indeed loved Jonathan as much as it is portrayed, I can't help but feel that his heart must have skipped a beat at the news. Mephibosheth! He *is* alive! He was not a victim of the Philistines. He *is* alive! To find Mephibosheth would almost be the same as resurrecting Jonathan, at least in David's heart and memory. Mephibosheth is alive!

My wife and I have very old and good friends who live in Tennessee. Gerry and I grew up together, his father having pastored the First Baptist Church in my hometown. We parted ways during our college years, and then reunited in seminary in Louisville, Kentucky. Gerry and Julie lived above us in an old house on Willow Avenue that had been converted into three apartments. We had our first children just a few months apart. We were present in the hospital when their son Kyle was born, and Gerry was present when our Emily came into the world. In fact, I will never forget that early morning when Gerry softly tapped on our back door. "Randy, Janet, it's time. We're going to the hospital." It was an exciting time for all of us, a time in our lives that bonded us together forever. We do not get to see our friends nearly as often as we would like, and we see their three sons even less. But Kyle will always hold a special place in our hearts because we were there when he was born. He is the first-born son of my good, good friend.

Did David feel the same way about Mephibosheth? We can't be certain, of course, but when told Mephiboseth is indeed alive, David asks immediately, "Where is he?" And Ziba says, "Oh, I heard he might be in one of the remote villages a few miles southwest of Hebron, but it might just be a rumor." No, that's not what he said at all, is it? Ziba was very specific about where Jonathan's son could be located. "He is in the house of Machir, son of Ammiel, at Lo-debar." It's surprising he didn't say, "You'll find him at 1723 Elm Street, two blocks north of the well, in the third apartment on the left." Ziba knew exactly where he was! Evidently the loyalty of Jonathan was visited upon the servants of Saul, and Ziba's knowledge of the whereabouts of Jonathan's son is a sign of that loyalty. Not everything in the house of Saul was bad. But David needed to know something before he persisted in his quest to find the youngest son of his late friend Jonathan. Mephibosheth is crippled.

Cripples were not looked upon kindly in those days. Today, we would refer to them as "physically challenged," but in the time of David they were purely and simply cripples. The general attitude, as was true in the days of

Jesus, was that people were crippled for a reason. Usually, that reason was God's vengeance. They, or their parents, had sinned, and now that sin was being visited upon the one bearing the infirmity. It would have made no difference that this crippled man had once lived in a house of royalty. A cripple is a cripple, no matter what. He is "an endangered species."[2]

When the encounter between David and Mephibosheth finally occurs, you can tell by his response to David that Mephibosheth suffers from low self-esteem. When David locates him and calls for him to come to Jerusalem that he might see the son of his late and good friend, and offers his kindness to him, Mephibosheth, on his knees and with his nose studying the cracks in the floor, says, "What is your servant, that you should look upon a dead dog such as I?" Think of how difficult it would have been for Mephibosheth, crippled in both feet, to get down on his knees before the king. He doesn't know why David has summoned him. For all he knows, David may be prepared to kill him. After all, a regime change has taken place, and his family is now deposed. As far as Mephibosheth knows, he may be as good as dead. "What is your servant, that you should look upon a dead dog such as I?"

"I'll tell you who he is," David says. "He is one who will eat at my table, and never live in fear again." And from that day on, Mephibosheth was treated, and loved, by David as if he were his own son.

"So David reigned over all Israel; and David administered justice and equity to all his people." It is a wonderful summary statement of the way David, as king, ruled his people. The story of his benevolence toward Mephibosheth illustrates David's sense of love and fairness. At no other time in his life was it more true: David was a man after God's own heart.

But David was also a man with a great deal of power, both personal and public. It was as true in David's day as it is ours…"Power corrupts. Absolute power corrupts absolutely." And David had his moments of corruption, as we all know. But there is an interesting epilogue to this story.

It is years later. Absalom, one of David's sons, leads a revolt against his own father. David has to flee for his life, and when he does, Ziba, the former servant of Saul, goes with him while Mephibosheth stays behind in Jerusalem. Ziba becomes a traitor to Mephibosheth by telling David that Jonathan's son has remained in Jerusalem out of loyalty to Absalom. And David believes him. If and when he ever gets back to Jerusalem, he will confront Mephibosheth over his apparent disloyalty.

If you know the story, you are aware that David defeats Absalom, who dies in battle by having his long hair caught in the fork of a tree limb. When

David returns to Jerusalem, Mephibosheth is able to tell him why he remained behind. He is crippled. In order to flee Jerusalem with David, he needed the assistance of Ziba who left him behind. Then, he tells David about Mephibosheth's supposed betrayal. One of them, Ziba or Mephibosheth, is not telling the truth. Who is David to believe? The narrator of the story doesn't tell us who is lying. He may not have known himself. But obviously, one of them is a liar. What is David to do?

Well, what would you do? Brand them both as liars and have them killed? It wouldn't have been the first time for David, and he certainly has the power to do it. Put yourself in his sandals. What would you have done? Well, this is what David does…He chooses to accept both men back into his household. Rather than respond to an either/or situation, he chooses to make it both/and. In today's terminology, we would say he made it a win-win situation by showing mercy to both. David doesn't want to know who is lying and who is being truthful. He simply accepts them both, out of a sense of grace and forgiveness, acceptance and kindness — and yes, power. It is as close to the gospel of Jesus Christ as anything you will find in the Old Testament. "David administered justice and equity to all his people."

There is an interesting note in this story from 2 Samuel that provides us a hint of what is going on. The narrator chooses to give us the names of those who served David on his political council. Remember Joab, the son of Zeruiah, the nephew of David, who would just as soon kill somebody as say hello? He is David's commander-in-chief. Zadok and Abiathar are priests while Seraiah is his secretary. Benaiah commands the bodyguards, and David's sons also serve as priests. Jehoshaphat, the son of Ahilud, is recorder. It is his responsibility to put down everything — everything — that happens during King David's life and reign over Israel. In fact, the Hebrew word for "recorder" could be translated *remembrancer*.[3] Jehoshaphat was David's remembrancer, and of all the stories he chose to use in illustrating David's rule of his people with justice and equity, he chose this one about Mephibosheth. The one story the "remembrancer" chose to record about this portion of David's life is the one that illustrates his loving and kind heart. "David administered justice and equity to all his people."

The issue of justice and equity is as old as humanity and as current as this morning's newspaper. Consider our seemingly ever-present political elections. The candidates discuss all kinds of issues: the economy, Social Security, education, guns, violence, war…Whatever it takes to make life better for America's citizens, they promise to do it. The spinmeisters work feverishly to make their respective candidates look as if they really and truly care for all the people of our country. And maybe they do. Maybe they do. But it seems to me that perhaps the one element missing from all the political rhetoric to which we constantly are exposed is the foundation of justice and equity. It is the basic idea of kindness.

However, it is not just missing in the political process. Listen to the people on the radio. Read the columnists in the newspaper or watch the political dialogue programs on television (but not on Sunday morning, please). What do you hear? Cynicism, skepticism, anger, rejection, suspicion, betrayal of common decency. We have lost, in many respects, our capacity for kindness.

Now, I realize there were probably many different and complex layers to the personality and leadership of David so many years ago. Nevertheless, this story can illustrate for us the level of kindness and love that is possible, if we will choose to live it. And if there is anyone in this country who should lead the parade of kindness, it is those who are committed to the One who, in the highest form of kindness, gave his life on the cross that we might know what self-giving love is all about.

We who bear the name of Jesus trade our spiritual birthright for a bowl of pottage if we leave it up to government solely to provide justice and equity in our land. That should not be a function solely of government. It should be the everyday reality of the people. It falls to all of us, in individual acts of kindness (whether random or not) and mercy and love and grace, to reflect the kindness and mercy and love and grace of our Lord Jesus Christ.

Did you notice the use of the word "reflect"? While it is vitally important that we be involved in the election process, and vote our conscience and our opinion, we must recognize that is not in our power as individuals or as a church or as a nation of people to generate righteousness or kindness or love. Only God can do that. The only thing we can do is reflect it. And the only way to do that is to be like David. Better yet, it is to be like his offspring Jesus. It is to have God's own heart.

So regardless of what your political leanings may be, recognize that our ultimate allegiance is to an unseen government Jesus called the kingdom of heaven. When we give our hearts to the One who has made this kingdom available to us, we will be his instruments of mercy and grace, and love and kindness...and there will indeed be justice and equity in the land.

Notes

[1]Eugene H. Peterson, *Leap Over a Wall* (Harper: San Francisco, 1997), p. 170.

[2]Walter Brueggemann, *Interpretation: First and Second Samuel* (John Knox Press: Louisville, 1990), p. 268.

[3]Robert Alter, *The David Story* (W. W. Norton & Company: New York, 1999), p. 239.

~ Ten ~
Sent

"It happened late one afternoon..." (2 Samuel 11:2).

The clan history of Scotland is fascinating. Prior to the Clearances in the late eighteenth and nineteenth centuries, when the English rid the Highlands of most of its inhabitants, there were three divisions of tenants. The tacksman (a "tack" was a form of lease), dealt directly with the landowner. Then there were the crofters, who often made informal lease arrangements with their landlords. The lowest rung on the social ladder belonged to the cottars, who were by far the largest in number.[1] They found themselves at the whims and mercies of their landlords, which proved eventually to be their undoing. In addition to the right to land use, landowners and/or clan chiefs, who were often both and the same, would provide protection for those who lived in their domain. In turn, the tenants would give their chiefs a certain amount of their time in military support. In fact, devotion to one's clan chief ran deeper than one's commitment to the king. Often, such conflicts occurred between clans, and when the chiefs needed military support, they found it in those who occupied and worked their lands. A more thorough study of this small nation's history reveals a quite violent past, and for many centuries this was the method by which society was ruled.

It was not unlike the way it was in David's day. David, once the active and warring king of Israel, has now reached the point in life when he has others to do his work for him. It is spring, the time of year when most kings "sally forth," as they say, to do battle with their enemies. But David has decided not to do so this year for reasons we do not know but can only conjecture. He's not getting any younger, you know. Besides, why risk his life when he has loyal and committed people to fight his battles for him?

Political and military devotion was tied into one's relationships. Take Joab, the son of Zeruiah, for example. The nephew of David is still a hotheaded mercenary. But the man sure knows how to fight, in a place and time when such skill definitely comes in handy. There were times, no doubt, when David was virtually apoplectic over Joab's violent shenanigans, but David would trust him with his own life. And Joab is as loyal to David as David is to him. It is true that Joab operates under the parameters of his own agenda, and rarely does David a favor without asking for something in return. But when push comes to shove, David knows he can count on Joab.

Right now, in this particular spring, Joab is leading David's troops against the rebellious Ammonites and their newly-crowned king, Hanun. David can picture in his mind just what strategy Joab will use in bringing the cocky Hanun to his knees, and instinctively knows that victory is assured. There's a side of David that wishes he were there, right in the midst of the battle. He could use the adrenalin rush, but common sense tells him it is better that Joab go to war without him. Being able to delegate authority is the mark of a strong leader, and despite the fact that it runs counter to his instincts, David gives in to his better judgment. In this particular spring, David has stayed home.

But David isn't happy when he's got nothing to do, and right now he's got absolutely nothing to do. He has finished his after-lunch siesta and it is now late afternoon, a good time to go up on the rooftop while the sun is low in the sky and the breezes are cool. He reflects upon what he has accomplished in life. Apart from this pesky little conflict with his neighboring Ammonites to the east, life couldn't be better. He has tribute coming in from other countries and his treasury is growing fat with the surplus. He now dominates all the world between the Nile River in Egypt to the south and the Euphrates River to the north. He is in control of the Aramaeans, the Syrians, and the Edomites. He is the chief of the Moabite tribes and has established treaties with Tyre and Hamath. Soon, very soon, Rabbah, the capital city of the Ammonites, will fall and his successes will be complete. History will look back and record that this was David's golden era.

But isn't it true that those who have "everything" never have enough? David has fame, possessions, family (a sign of God's blessing), control, power. David has lots and lots of power. All he has to do is snap his fingers and there will be twenty — nay, fifty — people at his beck-and-call. His goals are met and his dreams are fulfilled. There is nothing new under the sun.

But David is like the man who had, in his own words, arrived at the top of the mountain only to discover it was covered not with snow but with salt.

David is restless with his success. It isn't enough. He wants more.

I am reminded of the story of a woman who visited an elderly friend. They caught up on old times over afternoon tea, and had a delightful visit together. When it was time to leave, the younger woman said to her friend, "The next time I come, would you like me to bring you something?"

"Oh no," replied her friend. "I don't need anything else. It would just be something else to dust."

Well, David thinks he needs something to dust. What he has is not enough. What he has is *never* enough. And that is when he sees it — a flash of light. Actually, given a second look, he realizes it is light reflected…off what? David scans the city below and there, not that far away really, he focuses his eyes on what had fleetingly caught his attention. It takes a moment for him to settle in on the location, but finally he sees that it is light reflected off water, water used for bathing.

And that is when he sees her. She is beautiful. Oh, she is beautiful. And she is unclothed. David's heart flutters and his mouth turns dusty, gluttonous with lust. He knows instinctively and instantly that he has to have her. He has to have her soon. He has to have her now, right now. And since David is accustomed to getting what David wants — he is the king, you know — he sets in motion a chain of events that would change him and his life forever, as well as the lives of those around him.

David arranges not only a liaison with the woman, whom we know to be Bathsheba, but a child is conceived out of wedlock. There is more to the narrative, of course. In a convoluted story such as this, there is always more. Like an onion, the more you peel, the more there is. That is the steamy and sordid story of David and Bathsheba.

To cover up their misdeed, David attempts to manipulate Bathsheba's husband into thinking the child is his. But despite his best, and most devious efforts, it doesn't work. In desperation, David arranges with the crafty and ruthless Joab to have Bathsheba's husband Uriah killed in battle so David can take her to be his wife and give legitimacy to the birth of their child. David has to arrange all this quickly. Time, when a woman is with child — and it is not the child of her husband — is of the essence.

It is a story seemingly more fitted for Hollywood than the Old Testament. If discretion weren't called for, this could easily be turned into an R-rated tabloid. In fact, I find myself a bit uncomfortable explaining it to you as I have.

The heart of this story is found, not in what happens so much as how it happens. David uses his personal and public power to manipulate, lie, and yes, even murder. If you are into ranking sins, this one is definitely at the top.

Frankly, this is a David we wish we had never met. It is, without doubt, the blackest chapter in his life. Had we never heard this story before, it would sneak up on us with an explosive and demoralizing power. We would be tempted to put the book away and read no further. When idols fall, they fall hard and fast.

Up to this point, we had become familiar with a David who has grown in spiritual and emotional understanding, a David who governs his people with justice and equity, a David who has everything going for him and appears to be in intimate touch with the Source of such spiritual strength. We know David to be a man after God's own heart! How in the world could *our* David do such a thing? We take this personally! David is our hero! "We aren't prepared for such a David.[2]

There is a recurring word used in this story that provides us a clue as to what is truly going on here. Did you notice it? How David does such a thing is found in the simple, and seemingly harmless, word "sent." Yet, take this inane little word and think of how, when coupled with a manipulative heart, it can make for such disaster by tracking "David's descent from love and obedience into calculation and cruelty."[3]

Let's consider how the word "sent" is used to tell this story.

First of all, we are told that "David *sent* Joab"

"David *sent* someone to inquire about the woman."

"David *sent* messengers to get her…"

Sent, sent, sent. That is the first part of David's cunning and deceit. He has the personal and royal power to send anyone anywhere on any kind of mission his heart desires, and they have no choice but to respond. So David uses his power to send.

However, his transgression turns on him when we are told that he isn't the only one who sends. Bathsheba, we are told, has conceived David's child. "And she *sent* and told David, 'I am pregnant.'"

This news, which shouldn't have been so terribly startling to David, projects him into a second round of scheming and manipulating. "So David *sent* word to Joab, '*Send* me Uriah the Hittite.'" Now David has gotten others into the act of doing his dirty work for him. "And Joab *sent* Uriah to David." When Uriah doesn't fall for David's trickery (ironically, out of great devotion to his king who, behind the scenes is so ruthlessly plotting against him), "David wrote a letter to Joab, and *sent* it by the hand of Uriah." What, unwittingly, Uriah doesn't know is that the letter he is carrying in his hand includes instructions for his own death. Once the murderous deed is done, "Joab *sent* and told David all the news." "So the messenger went, and came and told David all that Joab had *sent* him to tell."

Uriah has died in battle at David's command, and when the proper time is over for Bathsheba to grieve the death of her husband (the sooner the better, as far as David is concerned), "David *sent* and brought her to his house, and she became his wife, and bore him a son." The son dies seven days after it is born. By this time, David knows God's displeasure of his terrible sin, for God always gets in the last word. In the following narrative, we are told that "The Lord *sent* Nathan to David." "You are the man!" Nathan says to David as he points his bony finger at the king. "Why have you despised the word of the Lord to do what is evil in his sight?" Recognizing what he has done, David repents. But life will never again be the same; not for David, king of Israel, a man after God's own heart, nor those who compose his clan.

Sent, sent, sent. The word *sent* has no power of its own, of course. It all depends on who is doing the sending and who is the one being sent. If you missed it the first time, do not let it slip by you this time. **God always gets in the last word!** And the last word is what John wrote in his first epistle: *"God sent His only Son into the world so that we might live through Him."* The final word always belongs to God.

The One God sent to us did not manipulate others so he might have anything his heart desired. The One God sent to us willingly died on the cross so God might have the final word in you and me. The final word is that "God *sent* His only Son, that we might live through Him."

Sent, sent, sent. In the hands of David, the word becomes dirty and defiled. In the hands of God, it is a word flooded with grace. Aren't we glad, then, that God always gets in the final word?

Notes

[1]P. A. MacNab, *Mull & Iona* (The Pevensey Press: Devon, England, 1995), p. 55.
  [2]Eugene H. Peterson, *Leap Over a Wall* (Harper: San Francisco, 1997), p. 183.
  [2]Ibid.

~ Eleven ~
Son of David

"Now these are the last words of David..." (2 Samuel 23:1).

"What do you think of the Messiah? Whose son is He?" (Matthew 22:42).

David, king of Israel, is grateful that he had appointed a good cabinet to assist him in the governance of the Hebrews. For years they have served him faithfully, and now he needs them more than ever. It is not because he needs to go fight battles and leave them in charge while he is absent. It is not because his kingdom has grown so extensively and the complexity of its leadership requires such help. David needs his colleagues because he has grown old, and he simply doesn't have the heart for it anymore.

David thinks of this as he shivers under the blanket his servant has draped over his shoulders. He is up on the roof of his palatial mansion. It has become, in these last years of his life, his favorite place to be. The cool afternoon breezes blow gently, and it is peaceful here. It is here he can think. It is here he can remember those golden, glory days when his body was strong and his will and determination even stronger. It is here that no one disturbs him, and David has come to the point in life when he doesn't want to be disturbed. Leave the leadership of the nation to his faithful cabinet members. Now, all he wants to do is remember the past while he still has a mind with which to be able to remember.

Funny, isn't it? This is where, years before, he had first set eyes on her...his beloved Bathsheba. She was married to Uriah then, but that didn't matter to David. He was at midlife, and nothing would stand in the way of his urges. He loved her the first time he saw her, and he loved her now. He had repented of his grievous sin in taking Bathsheba and arranging the death of her husband. But while he was honestly sorry for his impetuous action, he must admit that even after all these years he wasn't completely certain he regretted it. They had lost their first son, that is true, but later Solomon was born to them, and everyone knew that Solomon was David's best and strongest son. And, Solomon would be the next king. So, if the Lord God would forgive him the somewhat rebellious thoughts of an old man, he's not so sure that if he had it to do over again he would have done it any differently.

But most of all — most of all — in his old age David thinks of his God. What would his life have been like had God not reached down and put his touch on him? What would have become of the eighth son of Jesse? Remember Samuel? It's been so many years since Samuel, even then an old man, came to his home village of Bethlehem. His father's servants came looking for him while he was tending sheep. "They need you to come home," they had said to the young boy David. "Who will keep my sheep?" he protested. "We will stay with the sheep until you return," they promised. Funny…he never returned to the sheep, for Samuel anointed him that day, anointed him king of Israel.

Of course, he didn't assume the throne right away. There was the matter of a certain man named Saul. Saul was king of Israel, even though God's Spirit, God's blessing, had departed from him. But Saul wasn't willing to give up the throne. It would just be a matter of time, David supposed, before he would follow Saul in leading Israel, but what he didn't count on was Saul's intense hatred and jealousy toward him. David, now in his old age, recalls the years of hiding out in the wilderness, evading Saul's every move. *Do what you have to do. Just stay alive.* It was a mantra David had repeated to himself over and over in those heady, more desperate year. *Do what you have to do. Just stay alive.* How many times had he reminded himself that his day would come if he would only be patient and depend on the Lord?

Everything comes back to the Lord, doesn't it? No matter what he does, good or bad, everything — every thought, every deed — comes back to his consideration of the Lord.

David retraces in his mind the journey his life has taken him. From Bethlehem to the wilderness, from the wilderness to Hebron, from Hebron to Jerusalem.

And the relationships. David's eyes grow misty as he remembers Jonathan. Jonathan, his good, good friend whose life ended tragically on the same day as Saul met his demise. Much too soon. Jonathan died much too soon. Michal and Abigail, Bathsheba and Abishag. Oh, the women he had known.

And Absalom. "Absalom, my son, my son!" he had cried when he received word that Absalom had died, even though he did so in rebellion, trying to take David's kingdom away from him. Once again, especially now in his old age, the pitiful words continue to well up in his throat. "Absalom…"

Regrets? Oh yes. Who doesn't have regrets? Absalom, perhaps, being the greatest. But still, as he runs the finger of his memory along the map of his life, he knows it is how the Lord has wanted it. The Lord. Everything comes back to the Lord, doesn't it?

David calls for Seraiah, his secretary. He has some things he wants written down, for posterity. Kings do such things, you know. When Seraiah takes the chair across from him, David notices the gray in his hair and the slight tremor in his hand. My goodness! Seraiah is getting old too! And Jehoshaphat and Benaiah, even the rascal Joab. Joab has seen his last skirmish. "We all will pass soon, won't we?" David thinks. He says it not so much to himself but to someone else. Who? To the Lord. He is finding these days that his thoughts are not so much to himself as they are given to God.

Everything comes back to the Lord, doesn't it?

He isn't certain of it at the time, but his suspicion, nevertheless, is strong. This could be the very day the Lord takes him from his beloved Jerusalem, from Bathsheba and Solomon, from everything. He has called for Seraiah because he has something to say and he has a feeling these just may be his last words. He wants his testimony recorded, so he measures the words carefully with his shaky voice. It is an oracle I give to you, David says to his trusted secretary…

> *It is an oracle I give to you, I the son of Jesse.*
> *It is the oracle of the man whom God has exalted,*
> *for I am the anointed of the God of Jacob,*
> *the favored son of the Strong One of Israel:*
>
> *The Spirit of the Lord speaks through me,*
> *his word is upon my tongue.*
> *The God of Israel has spoken,*
> *the Rock of Israel has said to me:*
> *One who rules over people justly,*
> *ruling in the fear of God,*
> *is like the light of morning,*
> *like the sun rising on a cloudless morning,*
> *gleaming from the rain on the grassy land.*

Is not my house like this with God?
For he has made with me an everlasting covenant,
ordered in all things and secure.
Will he not cause to prosper all my help and my desire?
Will he not cause to prosper all my help and my desire?

It is now a thousand years later, and as our eyes focus on a scene recorded in the Gospel of Matthew, we find a group of men arguing. Actually, a number of men have ganged up on one man, Jesus the Nazarene. The gospel writer tells us that the group is composed of Pharisees. The way Matthew relates this encounter, and others like it, when the Pharisees confront their enemy, they do not do it alone. They are never alone; they are always gathered together. It seems that whatever bravery the Pharisees have, it comes from the group; they have no courage unless they have the numbers. It also seems they have no ability to defend their faith; to think, talk, act, do anything, unless they are gathered together.

Actually, Jesus has been wrangling for quite awhile with the Pharisees and their ideological cousins, the Sadducees. They've peppered him with questions — loaded questions — designed to uphold and sustain their limited understanding and view of scripture. At every turn, just when they think they've got him cornered, Jesus eludes their verbal grasp. Finally, he turns the tables on them by asking them a question. "What is your opinion concerning the Messiah? Whose son is he? Where does he come from? Come on, boys, let me know that you're thinking. After all, we've invested some time and energy here grilling one another. We might as well make something of it."

It is then they mention the name of David. The Messiah, they inform Jesus, is the Son of David. Do you think David could have imagined it: that after all these years — a thousand years! — he would still be held in such reverence? A man after God's own heart. It is true, that's what they called him.

But everyone knew about Bathsheba. Everyone knew of his failings, his tendencies toward violence. Everyone knew that David was hardly, hardly perfect. Yet, after all these years, their hope in the coming Deliverer is bound up in all that David was and all that David stood for. The Messiah would be the Son of David. Just think of it.

Now, you've got to understand that this isn't the first go-around between Jesus and the Pharisees. In fact, it has become the main item on their agenda: going after the Nazarene, asking him this, asking him that, trying to trick him into saying something embarrassing or doing something he would regret. It hadn't worked so far, but you've got to give them credit for trying. They haven't given up yet.

As far as they are concerned, this is an easy question to answer. The carpenter is pretty shrewd, and has proven himself to be a formidable opponent, but this will be a piece of cake. "The Messiah," they respond, "is the Son of David."

Wrong again. Wrong, wrong, wrong. Jesus cites the 110th Psalm as a prooftext that David himself referred to the Messiah as Lord. If David looked upon the future Messiah as his Lord, how could he possibly be his son? Once again, Jesus traps the Pharisees and reveals their lack of understanding of the scriptures. The Messiah is not so much the Son of David as he is David's Lord. Yet, look at how many times in the New Testament Jesus is referred to as Son of David. It is because they expected the Coming One to be a warrior like David, not a suffering servant.

Something was brought to my attention just recently which I had never thought of before. It is a simple thought, but often it is the simple ideas that are the most profound. *People who have nothing in common do not argue.* It does make sense, doesn't it? People who have nothing in common simply ignore one another. It is when people do have something in common, and there is a clash of wills or understanding or intention about what they hold in common, that an argument breaks out.

Democrats and Republicans argue because what they have in common is the desire to hold the same offices. They want control of the major seats of government as well as the local places of leadership. From president to local councilperson, what causes many a dispute is that not everybody is going to win an election. There are winners and there are losers, and until it is decided who wins and who loses, there will be disagreement.

People who have nothing in common do not argue. The next time you get into a disagreement with your spouse or family member, remember that the reason you are doing so is because you love each other. You hold common interests in your hearts.

It is an understatement to say that the Israelis and Palestinians are not getting along very well these days. Why? They want to occupy the same land. They affirm the same God and come from common lineages. They hold much in common.

And it is precisely because Jesus and the Pharisees have something in common that they are at each other's throats. They have a common heritage in which David is the central figure. They embrace the same scriptures. They worship the same God. So what do they argue about? The interpretation of scripture. Jesus and the Pharisees argue about where Jesus comes from. He certainly isn't acting like their kind of Messiah. So, if he's not acting like the kind of Messiah they're looking for, since they are the chief interpreters of scripture and know more about the Bible than anybody else, he cannot possibly be the Messiah. He cannot be the Son of David.

Wait a minute…Son of David. That doesn't make much sense to us, does it? This is a thousand years removed from David in time. Why would Jesus, or anybody else alive in his time, be referred to as the Son of David?

Well, sometimes people become bigger in our eyes once they are gone. No doubt that was true when it came to David. A thousand years after his death, David, as far as the Hebrews are concerned, was an even greater king that when he actually ruled Israel.

I remember making the remark to a colleague in 1980 that I thought history would be kinder to Jimmy Carter than his contemporaries. I think that is being borne out. It's certainly true of Ronald Reagan, and even Richard Nixon is beginning to rise in status.

After David's departure, his reputation began to grow even more than when he actively ruled Israel. "Saul has slain his thousands," the people sang, "but David his tens of thousands." And that was when he was alive. After his death his reputation continued to grow and grow, and as his reputation grew, so did the Hebrew belief in the coming Messiah. To the Jews, the Messiah would be the Son of David. What did that mean?

David's reputation among the people was as a warrior king who fought his way to the throne of Israel. He was David the fearless king, unafraid of any Ammonite or Philistine — even those nine feet tall! David was the fierce fighter. David was the conqueror. David was the king! As the Son of David, the Messiah, the Coming One, would enter the holy city of Jerusalem on his white steed and send the Romans heading for the hills, never to return. That was the hope — the constant, burning hope — of Israel.

And that, more than anything else, is what Jesus and the Pharisees argued about.

In the Semitic context, the term "son" does not necessarily have to link two people by blood. For the Jews to think of the Messiah as the Son of David, it was not required that he be a direct descendent, but that he embody the attributes of the one whose name he carries. However, Matthew and Luke, in their gospels, go to great pains to show that Jesus literally descended from

David. In their minds, Jesus fits the bill, both literally and figuratively.

But notice that Jesus isn't so quick to accept the title "Son of David." His point to the Pharisees is that David referred to the future Coming One as "Lord." Therefore, Jesus isn't David's son, he is David's Lord. Jesus isn't a warrior like David, he is a suffering servant. Jesus isn't a conqueror of the enemy, as David was; he conquers the human heart with self-sacrificial love.

But there is a sense in which Jesus was much like David. "Son of David" was a title often bestowed on Jesus and not just because of his genealogy. David's story anticipates Jesus' story. There is not one element of David's life — even the angry, devious, murderous, scheming side of David — that God did not use in working out his purposes through him. The same is true of Jesus, and the same is true of you and me.

If David teaches us nothing else, we learn that God has little to do with what Eugene Peterson calls "boutique" spirituality. There is to be a certain earthiness to our faith, and to have that is not only to follow in the spiritual steps of David, it is to understand Jesus more fully too. There is nothing grittier than fighting for your life in the wilderness, that is true. But how much truer is it to say the same about dying willingly on a cross? To follow the One who died there is not to have a limp faith but a faith that is exuberant, inspiring, encouraging, dynamic, gutsy and real. Both David and Jesus, the Son — the Lord! — of David had *real* faith.

I submit that this is a worthy spiritual goal for you and me: to have a real faith. It is not something we attain instantly, nor easily. It takes, at least, a lifetime. But it is worth the seeking.

And understand that it is not only found in church. In fact, it is more often found in the everydayness of our lives: going to the store or to the office, getting caught in rush-hour traffic, doing the laundry, raking the leaves, cheering your hometown team, eating your favorite meal or just having a bowl of cereal in the morning or a bologna sandwich at noon, sorting your mail, watching your favorite TV program, hugging your spouse, listening to the concerns of your children, reading a novel, visiting a friend, enjoying that first cup of coffee in the morning, taking a late afternoon walk, watching the rain fall, taking note of the early morning frost, listening to the birds sing, exulting in the smile of a child, ignoring the cheesy Christmas music at the mall…

You get the picture. God is in all of this, for this — for you and me — is life. And God is there, for as it was with David, it all comes back to the Lord.

One day we will all come to the end of our days, just as David did. Perhaps we too will allow the finger of our memory to trace the road map of our lives. And when we do, just like David, it will come back to the Lord, our Maker and Redeemer. David would be pleased, I think, to know we have used the example of his life to do just that. And Jesus, the Son of David, will say to us, "That is why I came to you, that you might be with me. Come to me, for you are one who is after God's own heart."